# Improving Your
# Spelling

# Improving Your
# Spelling

*Boost your word power and
your confidence*

**MARION FIELD**

**How To Books**

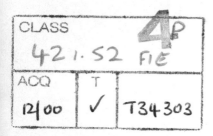
Published in 2000 by
How To Books Ltd, 3 Newtec Place,
Magdalen Road, Oxford OX4 1RE, United Kingdom.
Tel: (01865) 793806. Fax: (01865) 248780.
email: info@howtobooks.co.uk
http://www.howtobooks.co.uk

British Library Cataloguing in Publication Data.
A catalogue record for this book is available from
the British Library.

Cover design by Shireen Nathoo Design
Cover image by PhotoDisc
Cover copy by Sallyann Sheridon

Produced for How To Books by Deer Park Productions
Edited by Diana Brueton
Typeset by Kestrel Data, Exeter
Printed and bound by Cromwell Press Ltd, Trowbridge, Wiltshire

NOTE: The material contained in this book is set out in good
faith for general guidance and no liability can be accepted
for loss or expense incurred as a result of relying in particular
circumstances on statements made in the book. Laws and
regulations are complex and liable to change, and readers should
check the current position with the relevant authorities before
making personal arrangements.

# Contents

# Preface

English spelling is extremely complex because it owes so much to other languages. There *are* rules but unfortunately there are just as many exceptions to the rules. This book has been written in an attempt to help you sort out the problems. It gives examples of spelling variations and lists of frequently misspelled words as well as providing you with some fascinating background information on the origin of certain words.

There are chapters on forming plurals, hyphenating words, using apostrophes and discovering homonyms – words that sound the same but are spelt differently. There are also chapters dealing with the dictionary and the thesaurus – both indispensable tools for anyone who wishes to improve his or her spelling. Finally you will find a chapter on American spelling and one on jargon and slang.

At the end of most chapters there are exercises to help you practise what you have learnt. Suggested answers are given at the back of the book. It is hoped this book will be indispensable for those who wish to master English spelling.

*Marion Field*

# 1

## Identifying Different Sounds

English spelling is complex. There *are* some rules but these are often broken so the spelling of many words has to be learnt. Of the 26 letters in the alphabet, five are **vowels** and the rest are **consonants**. However there are other 'sounds' composed of combinations of letters. The vowels are a, e, i, o, u and all words have to contain at least one vowel. Some words use a 'y' instead, although 'y' is classed as a consonant.

Two vowels can be combined to make a single sound and these are known as **diphthongs** or **digraphs**. A consonant can also be used in a digraph but not in a diphthong.

### USING THE 'A' SOUND

An 'a' can be used alone between two consonants or combined with another vowel to produce a diphthong.

Short 'a' sound:

| | | | | | |
|---|---|---|---|---|---|
| bag | bap | brat | cat | fad | grab |
| lack | mass | mat | pad | lap | van |

For a long 'a' sound an 'e' is often added at the end of the word:

| | | | | | |
|---|---|---|---|---|---|
| cake | frame | lace | lane | mate | pale |
| sale | take | tale | tape | wake | wane |

### Using 'ai' and 'ay'

The combination of 'a' followed by an 'i' or 'y' produces a long 'a' sound:

| | | | | | |
|---|---|---|---|---|---|
| *ai*: | bail | bailiff | chase | claim | failure |
| | faint | faith | rail | rain | sail |
| | | | | | |
| *ay*: | affray | bay | day | delay | hay |
| | may | pray | relay | say | tray |

## Using 'ei'

The following words break the rule 'i' before 'e' except after 'c'; in this case the combination of 'e' and 'i' is pronounced as a long 'a' sound:

| | | | | |
|---|---|---|---|---|
| beige | deign | eight | feign | freight |
| feint | neighbour | rein | sleigh | veil | vein |

## Using 'ea' and 'ey'

In the following examples the 'ea' and 'ey' are both pronounced as long 'a' sounds:

| | | | | |
|---|---|---|---|---|
| *ea*: | break | great | | |
| *ey*: | convey | obey | prey | survey | they |

## USING THE 'E' SOUND

The 'e' is usually short when it is between consonants:

| | | | | | |
|---|---|---|---|---|---|
| bent | bet | deck | fed | fell | kept |
| wreck | | | | | |

By itself it usually has a 'long' sound as in the following:

| | | | |
|---|---|---|---|
| be | he | me | we |

## Using 'ea'

The diphthong 'ea' can produce a short 'e' sound as in the following:

| | | | | |
|---|---|---|---|---|
| bread | breath | death | endeavour | head |
| health | pheasant | pleasant | tread | wealthy |

In the following examples it has a long sound:

| | | | | | |
|---|---|---|---|---|---|
| beat | creak | flea | grease | heap | meal |
| meat | peach | peace | peak | peat | reveal |
| sea | seal | tea | teak | treat | veal |

## Using the 'ee' and 'ey'

A double 'e' and 'ey' can also produce long 'e' sounds:

| | | | | | |
|---|---|---|---|---|---|
| *ee*: | cheese | feel | free | peek | peel | reek |
| | sleep | sleeve | tee | | | |
| *ey*: | donkey | key | lackey | monkey | | |

### 'I' before 'e' except after 'c'

The following words contain a 'c' and therefore the 'i' follows the 'e':

| | | | | |
|---|---|---|---|---|
| ceiling | conceit | conceive | deceive | perceive |
| receipt | receive | | | |

The following words have no 'c' immediately before the vowels so the 'i' precedes the 'e' and follows the rule:

| | | | | | |
|---|---|---|---|---|---|
| believe | brief | chief | field | grief | niece |
| piece | priest | shield | shriek | siege | wield |
| yield | | | | | |

*Exceptions to the rule*

The 'i' follows the 'e' although there is no 'c' in the following words:

protein     seize     sheikh

### USING THE 'I' SOUND

There is a short 'i' sound when the 'i' is between two consonants:

| | | | | |
|---|---|---|---|---|
| bit | dig | fill | flick | hit | kick |
| sick | sit | stick | whip | | |

### Using 'ui'

A short 'i' sound can be produced when placing a 'u' before the 'i':

| | | | | |
|---|---|---|---|---|
| biscuit | build | guild | guillotine | guilt |
| guitar | | | | |

### Using the long 'i' sound

There is a long 'i' sound when there is an 'e' at the end of the word:

| | | | | |
|---|---|---|---|---|
| bite | hike | kite | site | spite | like |
| nice | rile | | | | |

### Breaking the rule with 'ei'

In the following words the rule of 'i' before 'e' except after 'c' is broken again and the 'ei' is pronounced with a long 'i' sound:

either     feint     feisty     geisha     height     neither

### Using 'igh' and 'ie'
The letters 'igh' and 'ie' also produce long vowel sounds as in 'eye':

| *igh*: | fight | light | right | sigh | sight | tight |
|--------|-------|-------|-------|------|-------|-------|
| *ie*:  | lie   | pie   | tie   |      |       |       |

## USING THE 'O' SOUND

There is a short 'o' sound when 'o' is between two consonants:

| box  | hop | god  | lob | lock | log |
|------|-----|------|-----|------|-----|
| long | pod | spot |     |      |     |

There is a long vowel sound when there is an 'e' at the end of the word:

| choke | hope | joke | lone | pole | spoke |
|-------|------|------|------|------|-------|

### Using the long 'o' sound in 'oa', 'oe', 'oo', 'ou' and 'ow'
The letter 'o' followed by an 'a', an 'e', another 'o', a 'u' or a 'w' can produce a long 'o' sound as in 'hope':

| *oa*: | boast   | boat    | coach        | coal   | coax       | foam  |
|-------|---------|---------|--------------|--------|------------|-------|
|       | goal    | groan   | oak          | road   | toad       | toast |
| *oe*: | doe     | foe     | hoe          | roe    | toe        | woe   |
| *oo*: | brooch  |         |              |        |            |       |
| *ou*: | boulder | mould   | soul         | though |            |       |
| *ow*: | barrow  | blow    | bow (weapon) |        | crow       | flow  |
|       | furrow  | grow    | low          | mow    | row (line) |       |
|       | sown    | swallow | tallow       | throw  | tow        |       |
|       | yellow  |         |              |        |            |       |

The three vowels, 'eau', can also produce a long 'o' sound. They derive from the French language and the plural form is sometimes an 'x' at the end of the word instead of an 's'.

| beau | gateau | tableau |
|------|--------|---------|

## USING THE 'U' SOUND

Short vowel sound as in:

| cup | duck | publish | suck | sup | up |
|-----|------|---------|------|-----|----|

### Using 'ou'

The vowels 'ou' can also be pronounced as a short 'u' sound:

| | | | | |
|---|---|---|---|---|
| double | couple | courage | flourish | rough |
| tough | young | | | |

## USING THE 'Y' SOUND

A 'y' is often pronounced as a vowel. It can be used to produce a short 'i' sound:

| | | | | |
|---|---|---|---|---|
| cyclamen | cynical | cyst | gymnast | hysterical |
| krypton | | | | |

In the following words it is pronounced as a long 'e' sound:

| | | | | |
|---|---|---|---|---|
| baby | happy | litany | literacy | lovely | puppy |

It can also produce a long 'i' sound:

| | | | | |
|---|---|---|---|---|
| by | byte | crucify | cycle | cyclone | dynamite |
| fry | hydrate | | | | |

## MAKING OTHER VOWEL SOUNDS

As well as the 'short' and 'long' sounds produced by the five vowels, other vowel sounds can be made by combinations of letters.

### Using the 'ar' sound as in 'car'

The digraph 'ar' and the combination of 'ear' can produce this sound:

| | | | | | | |
|---|---|---|---|---|---|---|
| *ar*: | bar | barter | card | cart | dark | darn |
| | embark | garter | hard | hark | mar | march |
| | partner | remark | | | | |
| *ear*: | heart | hearth | | | | |

### Using the 'air' sound

The following combinations of letters can all produce an 'air' sound: air, are, ear, eir:

| | | | | | | |
|---|---|---|---|---|---|---|
| *air*: | chair | fair | hair | lair | pair | stair |
| *ear*: | bear | pear | tear | wear | | |

| *eir*: | heir |  |  |
|---|---|---|---|
| *are*: | care | dare | mare |

## Using the 'ear' sound

'ear' and 'eer' can both be pronounced as 'ear':

| *ear*: | appear | beard | dear | hear | near | spear |
|---|---|---|---|---|---|---|
| *eer*: | beer | career | leer | queer | seer | steer |
|  | volunteer |  |  |  |  |  |

## Using the 'er' sound

A number of digraphs can be used to produce an 'er' sound as in 'her': ar    er    ir    or    our    re    ur:

| *ar*: | circular | grammar | nectar | particular | regular | sugar |
|---|---|---|---|---|---|---|
| *er*: | barter | berth | better | butter | cutter | garter |
|  | jerk | lawyer | mercy | merge | teacher | verse |
|  | wetter | writer |  |  |  |  |

| *ir*: | bird | dirt | fir | first | flirt | girdle | third | thirst |
|---|---|---|---|---|---|---|---|---|
|  | whirl |  |  |  |  |  |  |  |

| *or*: | actor | author | conductor | contractor | doctor |
|---|---|---|---|---|---|
|  | hector | inspector | instructor | professor | solicitor |
| *our*: | armour | colour | favour | glamour | humour |
|  | savour |  |  |  |  |
| *re*: | acre | centre | metre | sceptre | sombre |
|  | spectre | theatre |  |  |  |

| *ur*: | burn | burr | church | cur | curd | curtsey |
|---|---|---|---|---|---|---|
|  | curve | fur | furnish | hurt | lurch |  |
|  | murder | nurse | purse | slurp | turkey |  |

The letters 'ear' and 'our' can also produce an 'er' sound:

| *ear*: | earn | earth | heard | learn | search | yearn |
|---|---|---|---|---|---|---|
| *our*: | courteous | journal | journey | scourge |  |  |

## Using the 'ew' sound

The diagraphs 'ew' and 'ue' are pronounced as if there is a 'y' before it as in 'yew':

| *eu*: | chew | dew | few | hew | knew | pewter |
|---|---|---|---|---|---|---|
|  | spew | stew | steward |  |  |  |
| *ue*: | cue | due | hue | sue |  |  |

The letters 'ieu' and 'iew' also produce a similar sound:

| | | |
|---|---|---|
| *ieu*: | lieu | |
| *iew*: | review | view |

## Using the 'oo' sound as in 'too'

There are several combinations of vowels that make the 'oo' sound:

| | | | | | | |
|---|---|---|---|---|---|---|
| *ew*: | brew | crew | flew | threw | | |
| *oe*: | shoe | | | | | |
| *oo*: | bloom | broom | choose | croon | food | groom |
| | moo | mood | shoot | voodoo | zoo | |
| *ou*: | bouquet | group | soup | souvenir | through | |
| *ui*: | fruit | juice | recruit | | | |

## Using 'oo' as in 'book'

The 'oo' combination as in 'book' sounds halfway between a short 'o' and a short 'u' – a 'uh' sound:

| | | | | | |
|---|---|---|---|---|---|
| cook | crook | foot | good | rook | wool |

## Using the 'oi' and 'oy' sounds

These two digraphs are usually pronounced as in 'boy':

| | | | | | | |
|---|---|---|---|---|---|---|
| *oi*: | boil | choice | coil | coin | goitre | join |
| | loin | noise | point | soil | toil | voice |
| *oy*: | boy | coy | destroy | employ | joyful | loyal |
| | royalty | toy | | | | |

## Using 'ou' and 'ow' as in 'cow'

| | | | | | |
|---|---|---|---|---|---|
| *ou*: | about | aloud | bough | bounce | bound | found |
| | ground | grouse | hour | round | | |
| *ow*: | allowed | brown | crowd | crowned | down | |
| | drown | frown | powder | prowler | row (noise) | |
| | rowdy | town | | | | |

## Using the 'or' sound

The following digraphs produce an 'or' sound: al, au, aw, or, ou:

| | | | | | | |
|---|---|---|---|---|---|---|
| *al*: | call | chalk | fall | hall | recall | talk |
| | tall | walk | wall | | | |
| *au*: | applause | caught | daughter | distraught | fraught | |
| | naughty | slaughter | taught | taut | | |

| *aw*: | awful | brawl | caw | claw | dawn | draw |
|---|---|---|---|---|---|---|
| | fawn | flaw | lawn | lawyer | paw | pawn |
| | saw | shawl | yawn | | | |
| *or*: | before | bore | for | more | lore | torch |
| | torn | torpid | sorbet | sordid | sore | |
| *ou*: | bought | brought | thought | | | |

The 'or' sound is also produced by using three letter combinations: 'oar' and 'oor':

| *oar*: | boar | hoary | hoard | hoarse | roar |
|---|---|---|---|---|---|
| *oor*: | door | moor | poor | spoor | |

## Using the 'our' sound
The 'our' sound can also be made by 'ough' and 'ower':

| *our*: | flour | hour | scoured | sour |
|---|---|---|---|---|
| *ough*: | | bough | | |
| *ower*: | flower | tower | | |

## Making separate vowel sounds
Sometimes two vowels together are not pronounced as one sound but each vowel represents one **syllable** (single unit in a word). All the following words use two vowel sounds and have been divided into syllables for clarity:

| be.ing | de.i.fy | de.i.ty | do.ing | | |
|---|---|---|---|---|---|
| glac.i.er | ob.ed.i.ent | qui.et | re.in.force | re.i.ter.ate |
| sci.ence | spon.tan.e.ous | var.i.e.ty | | |

The word 'ga.ie.ty' has three syllables; the middle one contains two vowels but creates one sound

## CHECKING THE CONSONANT SOUNDS

There are more consonant sounds than there are letters in the alphabet.

## Using digraphs
A digraph is two letters – either consonants or vowels – which together produce a single sound. Following are some examples of consonant combinations:

| *ch*: | chain | chair | chase | cheat | choose | mischief |
|---|---|---|---|---|---|---|
| | torch | | | | | |
| *sh*: | shake | shell | shoe | shoot | shut | push |
| *th*: | path | pithy | the | these | though | thought |
| | throw | | | | | |

## Using 'tch'

Sometimes a 't' is added before the 'ch' but the pronunciation remains the same:

| crutch | ditch | hatch | hitch | hutch | pitch |
|---|---|---|---|---|---|
| witch | watch | | | | |

## Using 'ph'

The combination of 'p' and 'h' is usually pronounced as an 'f' sound:

| phone | phonetic | phoney | photograph |
|---|---|---|---|
| phosphate | phosphorescence | phosphorus | phrase |
| physics | | | |

## Using 'gh'

Using 'gh' at the end of a word is also often pronounced as an 'f' sound:

| cough | laugh | rough |
|---|---|---|

## Using consonants and vowel combinations

The combination of consonants and vowels can also produce specific consonant sounds.

## Using 'q'

Remember that 'q' is *always* followed by a 'u' and is usually pronounced 'kw':

| equal | equity | queen | quick | quiet |
|---|---|---|---|---|

## Using 'ion'

A 't' or 's' or 'sh' followed by 'ion' at the end of a word is usually pronounced 'sh':

| *tion*: | detention | information | mitigation | obligation |
|---|---|---|---|---|
| | plantation | pollution | sensation | station |
| | transition | translation | | |

| | | | |
|---|---|---|---|
| *sion*: | comprehension | confusion | decision | discussion |
| | division | erosion | impression | incision |
| | mission | occasion | passion | pension |
| | precision | profession | progression | session |
| *shion*: | cushion | fashion | | |

If the word ends in the sound 'ā-shun', nine times out of ten the ending will be with a 't' – 'ation':

| | | |
|---|---|---|
| accommodation | administration | creation |
| imagination | population | punctuation |
| relaxation | stimulation | transformation |

*Using 'cian'*
The ending 'cian' is usually used for a person's job:

| | | | |
|---|---|---|---|
| beautician | dietician | electrician | magician |
| musician | mathematician | optician | paediatrician |
| physician | politician | statistician | technician |

*Using 'tian'*
The 'tian' ending is used for only a few adjectives, usually formed from proper nouns and therefore written with a capital letter:

| | | | | |
|---|---|---|---|---|
| Alsatian | Dalmatian | Egyptian | Haitian | Martian |

## INTRODUCING SILENT CONSONANTS

Some consonants at the beginning of digraphs are not pronounced at all. Only the second letter is pronounced.

### Ignoring the 'g', 'k' and 'w'
In words that begin with 'gn' and 'kn' the 'g' and 'k' are silent:

| | | | | |
|---|---|---|---|---|
| gnarled | gnash | gnat | gnaw | gnocchi |
| gnome | Gnostic | gnu | | |

| | | | | |
|---|---|---|---|---|
| knack | knapsack | knave | knee | kneel |
| knell | knew | knickers | knife | knight |
| knit | knock | knoll | knot | know |
| knowledge | | known | knuckle | |

In words that begin with 'wr' the 'w' is also silent

| | | | | |
|---|---|---|---|---|
| wraith | wrap | wrangle | wreck | wrapper |
| wreak | wreath | wreathe | wreckage | |
| wrench | wrest | wrestle | wretch | wretched |
| wriggle | wright | wring | wrinkle | wrist |
| writ | write | writer | writhe | wrong |
| wrote | wrought | wry | | |

## Ignoring the 'p'

In a few cases the 'p' at the beginning of a word is 'silent'. The following letter is usually an 'n' or more often an 's':

| | | | |
|---|---|---|---|
| pneumatic | pneumonia | | |
| psalm | psalter | pseudo | pseudonym |
| psychedelic | psychiatry | psychic | psychologist |
| psychopath | psychotic | | |

## Ignoring the 'd'

A silent 'd' sometimes appears before 'g' when there is a short vowel sound before it:

| | | | | |
|---|---|---|---|---|
| bridge | budge | budgerigar | budget | dodge |
| fudge | grudge | | | |

A long vowel sound is usually followed by 'ge':

| | | | | |
|---|---|---|---|---|
| age | cage | page | rage | sage |

## Finding the soft 'c'

When 'e', 'i' or 'y' follows a 'c', the pronounciation is like an 's':

| | | | | |
|---|---|---|---|---|
| central | centigrade | centimetre | centre | centipede |
| cinch | cinders | cinema | cyanide | cybernetics |
| cynic | | | | |

All other vowels produce a 'hard' sound:

| | | | | |
|---|---|---|---|---|
| cat | care | cave | cavalry | coat | cute |

When adding 'ed' or 'ing' to a word ending in 'c', it is usually necessary to add a 'k' so that the 'hard' sound is retained:

| | | |
|---|---|---|
| mimic | mimicked | mimicking |
| picnic | picnicked | picnicking |
| traffic | trafficked | trafficking |

### Finding the soft 'g'

An 'e' following a 'g' usually but not always suggests a 'soft' sound:

| | | | | |
|---|---|---|---|---|
| age | cringe | gem | gender | genealogy |
| general | generation | gentle | geology | singe |

When a suffix is added, the 'e' at the end of the word is usually retained:

ageing  singeing

Other words are usually pronounced with a hard 'g':

| | | | | |
|---|---|---|---|---|
| gate | gaze | grate | grateful | gravel |
| grave | graze | grease | greed | |
| green | grey | guess | guard | guide |

In the following words the first 'g' is hard and the second is soft as it precedes an 'e':

garage  greengage  gauge

### CHECKLIST

- The five vowels, a, e, i, o, u can be 'long' or 'short'.

- A dipthong is when two vowels are combined to make a single vowel sound.

- A digraph is when any two letters are combined to make a single sound.

- The rule 'i' before 'e' except after 'c' can be broken.

- A 'y' is sometimes used instead of a vowel.

- Some consonants are 'silent'.

### PRACTISING WHAT YOU'VE LEARNT

1. Add either 'ei' or 'ie' to the following words:
   Bel..ve, br..f, c..ling, ch..f, dec..ve, ..ght, fr..ght, gr..ve, n..ce, n..ghbour, pr..st, prot..n, rec..ve, r..n, s..ze, sh..kh, sh..ld, v..l, v..n, y..ld.

2. Correct any wrong spellings in the following sentences:
   a. He opened the biskit tin but the biuscits were stale.
   b. Niether Jane nor her brother was aloud to go to the mach.
   c. She became histerical when her handbag was stolen.
   d. The docter was called when the child became ill.
   e. The hier to the throne visited the docks and wachted the frieght being wieghed.
   f. He found the comprehention in his exam paper easy but the translacion was more difficult.
   g. The opening of the new stashun was an impressive occation.
   h. The group was queit as the ice slid down the glasier.
   i. There was a spontanious burst of applause as the winer crossed the finishing line.
   j. The mach was abandoned as the pich was waterlogged.

# 2

## Checking Capital Letters

**Capital letters** are used for a variety of reasons and it is very important to identify the times when they are necessary.

### PUNCTUATING YOUR WORK

A capital letter is, of course, always used after a full stop to start a new sentence.
—The bridge was old and had to be replaced. Both rail and road traffic were disrupted for several days.

Capital letters are also usually used after question marks and exclamation marks.
—How long will the traffic disruption last? She has to travel to London next week.
—How disgraceful! We should have been told the road was closed to traffic.

### Writing direct speech

Direct speech is when words are enclosed in inverted commas to indicate what someone is saying. The first word of a person's speech always starts with a capital letter even if it is preceded by a comma.
—Tracy remarked, 'It's going to be a lovely day.'

If a question mark or exclamation mark is placed within inverted commas and followed by the person speaking, a capital letter is not used.
—'I was held up for two hours!' she exclaimed.
—'I don't believe it!' he exclaimed.
—'Why don't you drive to London?' asked Lucy. 'It's much quicker.'

Notice that both 'exclaimed' and 'asked' begin with small letters although they are preceded by an exclamation mark and a question mark. This is because the words are connected to the person who is speaking.

Remember that the personal pronoun 'I' is *always* written with a capital letter.

## Utilising other punctuation marks
A capital letter is not used after a comma, a semicolon or a colon.
—Because it was pouring with rain, the tennis match was postponed.
—She shuddered; there was a frightening atmosphere in the house.
—Your spelling is weak: you must learn the basic rules.

## USING PROPER NOUNS

A **proper noun** is the name of a person, place, institution or brand name. They are always written with capital letters:

| | | | |
|---|---|---|---|
| Anne | Ben | British Museum | Cooke |
| Denmark | England | Farnham | Guildford |
| Kellogg's | Persil | | |

Capitals are also used when there are two main words as in a street or a river:

| | | |
|---|---|---|
| Brecon Beacon | Castle Street | Forest of Dean |
| Heathrow Airport | High Street | River Thames |
| Table Mountain | Vale of Evesham | |

## Writing days and months
The days of the week and the months of the year should *always* be written with a capital letter:

| | | | |
|---|---|---|---|
| Monday | Tuesday | Wednesday | Thursday |
| Friday | Saturday | Sunday | |
| January | February | March | April |
| May | June | July | August |
| September | October | November | December |

It is not necessary to use capitals when writing the seasons of the year:

| | | | |
|---|---|---|---|
| spring | summer | autumn | winter |

## Forming adjectives from proper nouns

A capital letter is always used if an **adjective** is formed from a proper noun as in the following:

| Proper noun | Adjective |
| --- | --- |
| America | American |
| Denmark | Danish |
| England | English |
| France | French |
| Germany | German |
| Spain | Spanish |

## WRITING TITLES

Capital letters are always used for people's titles:

| | | | |
| --- | --- | --- | --- |
| Mr Grey | Mrs Brown | Miss Green | Ms White |
| Duke of Kent | Lady Jones | St Francis | Earl of Arran |

Capitals are also used for the main words in institutions:

| | | |
| --- | --- | --- |
| British Library | Conservative Party | Labour Party |
| London University | Royal Academy | St Mary's Church |
| St Paul's Cathedral | Surrey County Council | Tate Gallery |
| Victoria and Albert Museum | Woking Borough Council | |

When writing the title of books, plays, films, magazines, newspapers or songs, use capital letters for the main words:

| | | |
| --- | --- | --- |
| Bless this House | Brighton Rock | Gone with the Wind |
| Lettice and Lovage | The Merchant of Venice | |
| Shakespeare in Love | The Sound of Music | Streetcar named Desire |
| Tale of Two Cities | The Times | Woman's Own |

## USING GEOGRAPHICAL TERMS

If you are writing about a specific region use capital letters:
—There is some spectacular scenery in the *South West*.
—There is a lot of industry in the *North East*.
—Houses are very expensive in the *South East*.
—It was colder in the *North* than the *South*.

If you are using the terms as directions only, there are no capital letters and the words are hypenated if there are two:
—Gatwick Airport is *south-west* of London.
—Cornwall is *south* of Somerset.
—You travel *north* on the M1 to drive to Scotland.


## CHECKLIST

- Always use capital letters after a full stop.

- Don't use capital letters after a comma unless you are writing direct speech.

- Don't use capital letters after semi-colons or colons.

- Use capital letters after question marks and exclamation marks unless you are writing direct speech.

- Use capital letters for proper nouns, and adjectives formed from them.

- Use capital letters for titles and geographical locations.


## PRACTISING WHAT YOU'VE LEARNT

Correct the following sentences:

1. It was very cold. the crowds were hurrying home.

2. 'how are you?' She asked. 'i haven't seen you for ages.'

3. The roar of the planes grew louder; The boys covered their ears.

4. The english team lost the match.

5. Jobs in the north east are scarce.

6. She only used persil automatic in her washing machine.

7. The british museum was closed for renovation.

8. The group went on a trip on the river thames.

9. She sent a number of articles to *woman's own* but they were returned by the editor, ms jenny ashton.

10. The film *shakespeare in love* won seven oscars.

# 3

## Forming Plurals and Changing Verbs

To make a plural it is usually necessary to add an 's' to the word and to make no other changes.

### ADDING AN 'S'

Nouns that end in an 'e' usually only require an 's' to form a plural:

| | | | |
|---|---|---|---|
| bone | bones | plate | plates |
| case | cases | rate | rates |
| date | dates | resource | resources |
| envelope | envelopes | sale | sales |
| file | files | scene | scenes |
| game | games | shape | shapes |
| globe | globes | spice | spices |
| guide | guides | table | tables |
| house | houses | toe | toes |
| magazine | magazines | tree | trees |
| niece | nieces | wine | wines |
| nurse | nurses | | |

Many **nouns** that end in consonants are also made plural by adding an 's':

| | | | |
|---|---|---|---|
| block | blocks | pen | pens |
| book | books | pencil | pencils |
| brain | brains | plan | plans |
| colour | colours | seat | seats |
| desk | desks | stamp | stamps |
| director | directors | street | streets |
| doctor | doctors | ticket | tickets |
| girl | girls | torrent | torrents |
| letter | letters | victim | victims |
| light | lights | wheel | wheels |
| newspaper | newspapers | whisk | whisks |

## CHANGING OR KEEPING THE 'Y'

If a noun ends in 'y' and is preceded by a consonant, change the 'y' into an 'i' and add 'es' to make the plural:

| | | | |
|---|---|---|---|
| ally | allies | lady | ladies |
| baby | babies | library | libraries |
| berry | berries | lorry | lorries |
| body | bodies | penny | pennies |
| company | companies | pony | ponies |
| enemy | enemies | ruby | rubies |
| enquiry | enquiries | sky | skies |
| estuary | estuaries | society | societies |
| family | families | story | stories |
| ferry | ferries | tragedy | tragedies |
| fly | flies | | |
| gallery | galleries | | |
| glory | glories | | |

### Looking at the exceptions
Surnames ending in 'y' need only an 's' to make the plural:
– The *Perrys* are moving to Taunton.
– The *Doubtys* are holding a party.
   A carriage drawn by a single horse was known as a 'fly'. The plural of this is 'flys'.

### Keeping the 'y'
If the 'y' is preceded by a vowel, retain the 'y' and add 's' to make the plural:

| | | | |
|---|---|---|---|
| alley | alleys | attorney | attorneys |
| chimney | chimneys | covey | coveys |
| donkey | donkeys | key | keys |
| journey | journeys | lackey | lackeys |
| tray | trays | trolley | trolleys |
| spray | sprays | storey | storeys. |

## LOOKING AT WORDS ENDING IN 'O'

If the 'o' at the end of a word is preceded by a vowel, an 's' only is usually needed to form a plural:

| | | | |
|---|---|---|---|
| cameo | cameos | cuckoo | cuckoos |
| curio | curios | impresario | impresarios |
| oratorio | oratorios | patio | patios |
| radio | radios | rodeo | rodeos |
| stereo | stereos | studio | studios |
| taboo | taboos | tattoo | tattoos |
| video | videos | zoo | zoos |

## An 'o' preceded by a consonant

Unfortunately, when a consonant precedes the 'o', there is no definite rule to help you decide whether to add 's' alone or 'es'. The following words end in 'es'.

| | | | |
|---|---|---|---|
| buffalo | buffaloes | cargo | cargoes |
| halo | haloes | hero | heroes |
| echo | echoes | mango | mangoes |
| mosquito | mosquitoes | negro | negroes |
| potato | potatoes | tomato | tomatoes |
| tornado | tornadoes | torpedo | torpedoes |

The following words need only an 's' to make them plural:

| | | | |
|---|---|---|---|
| casino | casinos | concerto | concertos |
| contralto | contraltos | dynamo | dynamos |
| embryo | embryos | libretto | librettos |
| manifesto | manifestos | photo | photos |
| memo | memos | solo | solos |
| soprano | sopranos | | |

## DISCOVERING DIFFICULT PLURALS

With some words you will find it necessary to add 'es' because the word would be difficult to pronounce without the addition of the 'e'. 'Es' has to be added to words ending in 's', 'ch', 'sh', 'x' and 'z':

| | | | |
|---|---|---|---|
| ass | asses | brass | brasses |
| cross | crosses | duchess | duchesses |
| grass | grasses | pass | passes |
| princess | princesses | witness | witnesses |
| bench | benches | church | churches |
| crutch | crutches | dispatch | dispatches |
| hutch | hutches | leech | leeches |
| lunch | lunches | porch | porches |

| | | | |
|---|---|---|---|
| torch | torches | trench | trenches |
| witch | witches | | |
| brush | brushes | bush | bushes |
| crash | crashes | crush | crushes |
| dash | dashes | flush | flushes |
| box | boxes | cox | coxes |
| fix | fixes | fox | foxes |
| hoax | hoaxes | | |
| buzz | buzzes | fizz | fizzes |
| waltz | waltzes | | |

## KEEPING OR CHANGING THE 'F'

If a noun ends in 'f', in some cases you will only need to add an 's' as in the following:

| | | | |
|---|---|---|---|
| brief | briefs | chef | chefs |
| chief | chiefs | cliff | cliffs |
| dwarf | dwarfs | handkerchief | handkerchiefs |
| muff | muffs | proof | proofs |
| roof | roofs | staff | staffs |

### Changing to 'ves'

Other nouns require you to change the 'f' to 'v' and add 'es':

| | | | |
|---|---|---|---|
| calf | calves | half | halves |
| knife | knives | leaf | leaves |
| life | lives | loaf | loaves |
| scarf | scarves | sheaf | sheaves |
| shelf | shelves | yourself | yourselves |
| wife | wives | wolf | wolves |

## MAKING PLURALS

### Making plurals of hyphenated words

A **hyphen** is a dash placed between two words that are closely linked. In most cases the 's' is added to the second word as in the following:

| | | | |
|---|---|---|---|
| back-bencher | back-benchers | by-law | by-laws |
| corner-stone | corner-stones | ear-ring | ear-rings |
| fun-fair | fun-fairs | hair-line | hair-lines |

| | | | |
|---|---|---|---|
| hair-style | hair-styles | head-dress | head-dresses |
| heart-break | heart-breaks | kick-off | kick-offs |
| knick-knack | knick-knacks | notice-board | notice-boards |
| post-mortem | post-mortems | press-stud | press-studs |
| set-up | set-ups | wage-earner | wage-earners |
| waiting-room | waiting-rooms | | |

In the following words the 's' is added to the first word because it is the most important:

| | | | |
|---|---|---|---|
| court-martial | courts-martial | lady-in-waiting | ladies-in-waiting |
| passer-by | passers-by | mother-in-law | mothers-in-law |
| sister-in-law | sisters-in-law | | |

When 'ful' is added to a word, the 's' is usually placed after it:

bucketfuls    fistfuls    handfuls        pocketfuls        spoonfuls

## Keeping the same word for the plural
In some cases the same word is used for both the singular and the plural as in the following:

deer        deer                    sheep        sheep

## Changing the word
Some words do not require an 's' to form the plural: the word itself changes.

| | | | |
|---|---|---|---|
| child | children | foot | feet |
| goose | geese | louse | lice |
| man | men | mouse | mice |
| tooth | teeth | woman | women |

## Using foreign words
As many English words are derived from foreign languages, particularly French and Latin, you will have to adapt the endings accordingly. Words ending in 'eau' usually derive from French and the plural has an 'x' added instead of an 's':

| | | | |
|---|---|---|---|
| bureau | bureaux | chateau | chateaux |
| gateau | gateaux | tableau | tableaux |

Latin words which end in 'um' usually change to 'a' for the plural:

| | | | |
|---|---|---|---|
| addendum | addenda | crematorium | crematoria |
| curriculum | curricula | datum | data |
| erratum | errata | | |

'Is' often becomes 'es':

| | | | |
|---|---|---|---|
| analysis | analyses | axis | axes |
| basis | bases | crisis | crises |
| oasis | oases | metamorphosis | metamorphoses |
| parenthesis | parentheses | synopsis | synopses |

'On' often becomes 'a':

| | | | |
|---|---|---|---|
| criterion | criteria | phenomenon | phenomena |

'Us' can become an 'i':

| | | |
|---|---|---|
| cactus | cacti | calculus calculi |

## ALTERING A VERB

A **verb** is a 'doing' or a 'being' word. The 'being' verb is 'to be'. To remind you, the past and present tenses of the verb 'to be' are set out below.

| Present tense | Past tense |
|---|---|
| I am | I was |
| you are | you were |
| he, she, it is | he, she, it was |
| we are | we were |
| they are | they were |

Some 'doing' verbs are: to bury, to dance, to play, to run, to spray, to write. As when making a plural, verbs also change their form when changing tense.

### Coping with the 'y'

Some verbs end in 'y' and sometimes, to change tense, you may have to add other letters. If there is a consonant before the 'y', change the 'y' into an 'i' before adding the other letters. However, you need to keep the 'y' before adding 'ing' as a double 'i' is very rare in English spelling. Some verbs that follow this pattern are:

accompany    bury      copy      glory      marry
occupy       remedy    worry

*Examples*
—When will she *marry*?
—She was *married* yesterday.
—Did he *copy* the answers?
—He *copied* her work.
—We must *bury* the treasure before the enemy come.
—They *buried* the treasure under the old oak tree.
—He will *worry* if I am late.
—She is *worrying* about her daughter.

If there is a vowel before the 'y', it is not usually necessary to change it. Add the letters after it.

*Examples*
—It was necessary to *spray* the crops.
—He *sprayed* the crops.
—She loves to *play* with her baby sister.
—She *played* with her baby sister.
—He is *playing* the piano.

*Exceptions*
As usual there are exceptions! The 'y' is sometimes replaced by 'i' as in the following examples:

| pay | paying | *but* | paid |
| lay | laying | *but* | laid |
| say | saying | *but* | said |

Other exceptions do the opposite! In the following cases where verbs end in 'ie', it is necessary to replace the two vowels with 'y'.

| die | dying |
| lie | lying |
| tie | tying |
| vie | vying |

## CHECKLIST

- A plural is usually made by adding 's' to words ending in 'e' or a consonant.

- Change the 'y' into 'i' and add 'es' if a consonant precedes the vowel.

- Keep the 'y' if a vowel precedes it.

- In some cases 'f' changes to 'v' before adding 'es'.

- Add the 's' at the end of hyphenated words except in certain cases.


## PRACTISING WHAT YOU'VE LEARNT

1. What is the plural of the following words?

| | | | | |
|---|---|---|---|---|
| alley | ally | baby | chimney | company |
| doctor | donkey | enemy | enquiry | file |
| journey | key | lackey | niece | nurse |
| pencil | pony | ruby | scene | sky |
| spray | storey | story | ticket | tragedy |
| tray | trolley | victim | whale | wheel |
| whisk | | | | |

2. Correct any mistakes in the following sentences:
   a. The soldiers were told their court-martials were to be held the following day.
   b. Comedians often make jokes about their mother-in-laws.
   c. The passer-bys ignored the speaker on his soap-box.
   d. All the farmers' wifes cut off the mouses' tails.
   e. The thiefs took the knifes from the waiting-roomes.
   f. The leafs turn brown in the autumn and the sheafs of wheat are harvested.
   g. The wolfs chased the childs who were in fear of their lifes.
   h. The sopranoes and the contraltoes were late for the concert because they couldn't find their librettoes.
   i. There were two tornados in quick succession.

3. Put the following sentences into the past tense:
   a. She (glory) in her misdemeanours.
   b. The examiner (remedy) the mistake.
   c. The mother (worry) because her daughter was late home.
   d. The victims of the plague were (bury) in a mass grave.
   e. Her brother (accompany) her to the audition.
   f. They were (marry) last year.

# 4

## Using Prefixes, Suffixes and Hyphens

A **prefix** is a group of letters placed before a word to qualify its meaning while a **suffix** appears at the end of a word. A hyphen is a dash placed between two words to link them. In some cases you have a choice. You may use a hyphen or you may join the two words into one. A hyphen may also be used between a prefix or a suffix and the main word.

### STARTING WITH A PREFIX

There are a number of prefixes which sometimes but not always require a hyphen before the main word. Some of these are 'ante-', 'anti-', 'bi-' and 'by'.

### The prefix 'ante-'
'Ante-' means 'before': following are some words that require a hyphen between the two branches of the word:

| | | |
|---|---|---|
| ante-room | ante-mortem | ante-post |

Words that do *not* need a hyphen with this prefix are:

| | | | |
|---|---|---|---|
| antecedent | antechamber | antechapel | antedate |
| antediluvian | antemeridian | antenatal | |

The words 'antenna' and 'antelope' start with the same letters but the 'ante' does not mean 'before' as in the previous examples.

### The prefix 'anti-'
The prefix 'anti-' means against and is used to suggest opposition to the main word. The following words use a hyphen between the prefix and the root words:

| | | | |
|---|---|---|---|
| anti-aircraft | anti-apartheid | anti-gravity | anti-hero |
| anti-novel | anti-Semite | anti-racial | |

There are more words that do not require a hyphen:

| | | | |
|---|---|---|---|
| antibiotic | antibody | antichrist | antichristian |
| anticlimax | anticlockwise | anticyclone | antidote |
| antifreeze | antipope | antiseptic | antisocial |
| antistatic | antitheses | | |

## The prefix 'bi-'
'Bi' means two or twice and words starting with 'bi' do not usually need hyphens:

| | | | |
|---|---|---|---|
| biannual | biathlon | biaxial | bicarbonate |
| bicentenary | biceps | bicultural | bicuspid |
| bicycle | biennial | bifurcate | bilateral |
| bilingual | bimonthly | binary | binoculars |

The following do use a hyphen:

bi-weekly            bi-yearly

## The prefix 'by-'
'By' suggests something that is secondary or incidental to the root word. The following words require hyphens:

| | | | |
|---|---|---|---|
| by-blow | by-election | by-lane | by-play |
| by-product | by-road | by-law | |

You do not need a hyphen in the following words:

| | | | |
|---|---|---|---|
| bygone | byline | bypass | bypath |
| bystander | byway | byword | |

## The prefix 'co-'
When using the prefix 'co-', a hyphen is usually used for convenience if the root word – usually a verb or its noun derivative – begins with an 'o':

| | | |
|---|---|---|
| co-operate | co-operation | co-opt | co-operative |
| co-ordinate | co-ordination | co-ordinator | |

It is also used when the meaning might not be clear as in the following:

co-belligerent            co-respondent

If the root word is a noun and the 'co-' is used to denote joint participation, a hyphen is usually used:

| | | |
|---|---|---|
| co-author | co-driver | co-signatory |
| co-pilot | co-star | |

A hyphen is not required in the following words:

| | | | |
|---|---|---|---|
| coagulate | coalesce | coalition | coeducation |
| coefficient | coequal | coexist | |

### The prefix 'counter-'
The prefix 'counter-' is used to suggest opposition. The following words require hyphens:

| | | |
|---|---|---|
| counter-attack | counter-attraction | counter-claim |
| counter-culture | counter-espionage | counter-intelligence |
| counter-productive | counter-reformation | counter-revolution |
| counter-sign | counter-tenor | |

The following words are written as one word:

| | | |
|---|---|---|
| counteract | counterbalance | counterblast |
| countercharge | counterfeit | counterfoil |
| countermand | countermarch | countermeasure |
| countermine | counterpoint | |

### The prefix 'cross-'
The following words require a hyphen:

| | | | |
|---|---|---|---|
| cross-bearer | cross-bench | cross-bones | cross-breed |
| cross-check | cross-country | cross-cultural | cross-cut |
| cross-dating | cross-examine | cross-eyed | cross-fertilise |
| cross-fire | cross-grain | cross-keys | cross-legged |
| cross-over | cross-patch | cross-piece | |

The following words are written as one word:

| | | | |
|---|---|---|---|
| crossbar | crossbill | crossbow | crossroads | crossword |

### The prefix 'de-'
The prefix 'de-' indicates a move away from or to undo something. The hyphen is usually used only when the root word begins

with a vowel and there might be confusion without it as in the following:

| | | |
|---|---|---|
| de-escalate | de-ice | de-aerate |

The following words do not require a hyphen:

| | | | |
|---|---|---|---|
| deactivate | debrief | decaffeinated | decapitate |
| decolonise | deceased | decentralise | declare |
| decompose | deduct | defend | defuse |
| defamation | degeneration | degrade | dehydration |
| delouse | denude | demerit | demoralise |
| deodorant | depend | depopulate | depressurise |
| deride | desegrate | dethrone | devolution |

## The prefix 'dis-'

This prefix can be added to a word to produce the opposite meaning:

| | | | |
|---|---|---|---|
| able | disable | arm | disarm |
| appear | disappear | believe | disbelieve |

## The prefix 'ex-'

The prefix 'ex-' meaning 'out' is not usually followed by a hyphen. An exception is 'ex-directory'. When the prefix is linked to a noun and means 'former', as in the following, a hyphen is used:

| | | | |
|---|---|---|---|
| ex-captain | ex-chairman | ex-convict | ex-headmistress |
| ex-husband | ex-minister | ex-serviceman | ex-sailor |
| ex-soldier | ex-wife | | |

## Separating the prefix

In a few cases where 'ex' precedes a word of Latin origin, the prefix is separated from the root word and no hyphen is needed:

| | |
|---|---|
| ex anima | from the mind – earnestly |
| ex cathedra | with authority, as from the Pope |
| ex curia | out of court |
| ex gratia | voluntary |
| ex hypothesis | by hypothesis |
| ex lege | arising from the law |
| ex parte | one sided |
| ex post facto | after the fact |
| ex voto | an offering made as a result of a vow |

### The prefix 'extra-'

The prefix 'extra-' suggests something 'outside' the root word and usually requires a hyphen:

| | | |
|---|---|---|
| extra-curricular | extra-marital | extra-sensory |
| extra-vehicular | | |

### The prefix 'far-'

The prefix 'far-', which suggests distance of space or time, requires a hyphen in the following words:

| | | | |
|---|---|---|---|
| far-away | far-famed | far-fetched | far-flung |
| far-off | far-out | far-reaching | far-seeing |
| far-sighted | | | |

### The prefix 'il-'

The prefix 'il-' is usually used with words beginning with 'l' to express the opposite. Remember that the negative word will have a double 'l'.

| | | | |
|---|---|---|---|
| legal | illegal | legitimate | illegitimate |
| logical | illogical | legible | illegible |
| liberal | illiberal | literate | illiterate |

### The prefix 'im-'

The prefix 'im-' is usually used before root words beginning with the following letters: b, m, p:

| | | | |
|---|---|---|---|
| balance | imbalance | material | immaterial |
| mature | immature | mobile | immobile |
| modest | immodest | moral | immoral |
| mortal | immortal | partial | impartial |
| passable | impassable | passive | impassive |
| patient | impatient | perfect | imperfect |
| personal | impersonal | pious | impious |
| polite | impolite | possible | impossible |
| practical | impractical | probable | improbable |
| proper | improper | prudent | imprudent |

### The prefix 'ir-'

The prefix 'ir-' is used before root words starting with 'r':

| | | | |
|---|---|---|---|
| rational | irrational | reconcilable | irreconcilable |
| regular | irregular | relevant | irrelevant |

| religious | irreligious | resolute | irresolute |
|---|---|---|---|
| respective | irrespective | responsible | irresponsible |
| reverent | irreverent | reversible | irreversible |

## The prefix 'in-'

The prefix 'in-' expresses inclusion within space, time or circumstances; it is used as a prefix in many words and in most cases a hyphen is not used. It is, however, required in the following words:

| in-built | in-depth | in-group | in-house | in-swing |
|---|---|---|---|---|
| in-tray | in-law | in-patient | | |

In some words 'in' can suggest the opposite to the root word as in the following where no hyphens are required:

| indiscipline | inedible | insane | inseparable |
|---|---|---|---|
| insignificant | insoluble | invisible | |

*Exception*

A notable exception to the above rule is the word *invaluable* which means the opposite to *not valuable*. It is in fact *very valuable* indeed. A price cannot be placed upon it.

## The prefix 'mis-'

The prefix 'mis-' suggests a negative and is often added to suggest the opposite of the root word:

| alliance | misalliance | align | misalign |
|---|---|---|---|
| apply | misapply | appropriate | misappropriate |

## The prefix 'neo-'

The prefix 'neo-' refers to something that is new or revived from an earlier period. It is often added to the reviving of certain philosophies or historical periods whose art or ideas have been revived. In these cases a hyphen is usually added:

| neo-classical | neo-colonial | neo-Hellenism |
|---|---|---|
| neo-Platonism | neo-scholasticism | neo-Nazism |
| neo-Victorianism | | |

The following words do not need a hyphen:

| neologism | the coining of new words |
| neophyte | new convert or newly ordained priest (mainly Roman Catholic) |
| neolithic | stone age |

## The prefix 'non-'

'Non-', which forms the opposite of the root word when added as a prefix, usually requires a hyphen:

| | | |
|---|---|---|
| non-acceptance | non-aggression | non-alcoholic |
| non-alignment | non-appearance | non-attendance |
| non-belligerent | non-combatant | non-commissioned |
| non-committed | non-compliance | non-delivery |
| non-essential | non-event | non-existent |
| non-fiction | non-flammable | non-human |
| non-fulfilment | non-interference | non-member |
| non-observance | non-playing | non-operational |
| non-professional | non-productive | non-returnable |
| non-slip | non-smoking | non-starter |
| non-stick | non-uniform | non-verbal |
| non-violence | | |

Some words which do not need a hyphen are:

| | | |
|---|---|---|
| nonagenarian (someone in their nineties) | | nonchalant |
| nonconformist | nondescript | nonentity |
| nonsense | | |

## The prefix 'off-'

The prefix 'off-' is sometimes followed by a hyphen as in the following:

| | | | |
|---|---|---|---|
| off-beat | off-glide | off-key | off-load |
| off-peak | off-putting | off-stage | off-licence |
| off-centre | off-day | off-season | off-time |
| off-year | | | |

The following words do not need a hyphen:

| | | | | | |
|---|---|---|---|---|---|
| offdrive | offprint | offset | offshore | offshoot | offside |
| offspring | offstreet | | | | |

*Exception*
'Off white' is written as two words.

### The prefix 'on-'

The following require a hyphen:

on-off        on-licence        on-line        on-stage        on-street

Hyphens are not required in the following words:

oncoming        ongoing        onlooker        onrush        onset
onside        onslaught

### The prefix 'over-'

The following words require a hyphen:

over-abundance    over-active    over-anxious    over-blown
over-burden       over-careful   over-confident  over-land
over-populate     over-react     over-sensitive  over-sexed
over-simplify     over-subscribe

The following words do not require a hyphen:

overact        overall        overate        overarm
overawe        overbalance    overbearing    overblouse
overboard      overcast       overcoat       overcrowded
overdo         overdress      overeat        overhaul
overhear       overjoyed      overlord       overshadow
oversight      oversleep      overtime       overvalue
overwhelm      overwork

### The prefix 'pre-'

'Pre-' means before and the prefix is sometimes followed by a hyphen but not always:

pre-arrangement  pre-cast       pre-Christian   pre-condition
pre-cook         pre-date       pre-elect       pre-engagement
pre-establish    pre-exist      pre-heat        pre-menstrual
pre-millennial   pre-natal      pre-prandial    pre-ordain
pre-pack         pre-Raphaelite pre-record      pre-tax
pre-school       pre-select     pre-set         pre-sharing
pre-stress       pre-war

The following words do not require a hyphen:

preamble       precaution     precede        precedence
precept        predecessor    precursor      prehistory
preoccupy      prescribe

### The prefix 'post-'

'Post', meaning 'after', is sometimes followed by a hyphen but there are a number of words that do not require it.

*Words requiring a hyphen*

| | | |
|---|---|---|
| post-box | post-classical | post-haste |
| post-Impressionism | post-mortem | post-paid |
| post-war | | |

*Words not requiring a hyphen*

| | | | |
|---|---|---|---|
| postcare | postgraduate | posthorn | posthumous |
| postmaster | postmistress | postnatal | postoffice |
| postposition | postprandial | postscript | |

### The prefix 'pro-'

This prefix is not usually followed by a hyphen:

| | | | |
|---|---|---|---|
| probate | probation | probity | problem |
| proceed | process | proclaim | proconsul |
| procreate | procurator | progression | prohibit |
| pronoun | protest | protract | protrude |

If 'pro-' is used in the sense of substitution or supporting, there is usually a hyphen:

| | | | |
|---|---|---|---|
| pro-cathedral | pro-proctor | pro-Labour | pro-Market |

### The prefix 're-'

This means doing something again. The hyphen is usually used if the root word begins with an 'e' so that pronunciation is not confused:

| | | | | |
|---|---|---|---|---|
| re-echo | re-edit | re-educate | re-elect | re-emerge |
| re-enact | re-enforce | re-establish | re-examine | re-export |

A hyphen is also sometimes used when forming a compound word. This is to avoid confusion as the word would change meaning if there was no hyphen. Look at the following examples; the words on the left have a different meaning from those on the right.

| | |
|---|---|
| react | re-act |
| recover | re-cover |

| | |
|---|---|
| reform | re-form |
| resign | re-sign |
| recede | re-cede |
| recount | re-count |
| recreate | re-create |

When an 'a' or a consonant follows the prefix, no hyphen is usually required:

| | | | |
|---|---|---|---|
| reappear | reappoint | reappraisal | rearrange |
| reascend | reassure | rebaptise | rebind |
| rebound | rebut | recapitulate | recant |
| recompense | recommit | reconcile | reconnaissance |
| recoup | | | |

## The prefix 'self-'

The prefix 'self-' which refers to acting of one's own accord is usually followed by a hyphen:

| | | |
|---|---|---|
| self-abuse | self-addressed | self-affirmation |
| self-aggrandisement | self-analysis | self-appointed |
| self-assertive | self-coloured | self-confident |
| self-conscious | self-educated | self-esteem |
| self-examination | self-explanatory | self-importance |
| self-reliant | self-sacrifice | self-satisfied |
| self-service | self-starter | self-supporting |
| self-taught | self-willed | |

*Exceptions*
The following words require no hyphen:

selfsame       selfless

## The prefix 'semi-'

The prefix 'semi-', meaning half, sometimes requires a hyphen and at other times does not.

*Words needing a hyphen*

| | | |
|---|---|---|
| semi-automatic | semi-bold | semi-chorus |
| semi-civilised | semi-detached | semi-furnished |
| semi-invalid | semi-official | semi-permanent |

*Words not requiring a hyphen*

| | | | |
|---|---|---|---|
| semibreve | semicircle | semicolon | semifinal |
| semitone | semiprecious | semitransparent | semitropical |
| semiquaver | | | |

## The prefix 'sub-'

This denotes a lower position. Some words that require a hyphen are:

| | | | |
|---|---|---|---|
| sub-edit | sub-editor | sub-branch | sub-machine-gun |
| sub-plot | sub-lieutenant | | |

Words that do not require a hyphen are:

| | | | |
|---|---|---|---|
| subaltern | subcontinent | subcontract | subculture |
| subdeacon | subdivide | subdue | subject |
| subjugate | subjunctive | subkingdom | submarine |
| sublimate | submit | subnormal | subordinate |
| subscribe | substitute | subtitle | subway |

## The prefix 'un-'

The prefix 'un-' suggests the opposite meaning to the root word:

| | | |
|---|---|---|
| unabridged | unaccompanied | unaccomplished |
| unadorned | unannounced | unattached |
| unaware | unbroken | unclean |
| uncluttered | uncomfortable | unconscious |
| uncrowned | undamaged | unhappy |
| unguarded | unhealthy | unhooked |
| uninspired | unlaced | unleashed |

## The prefix 'under-'

This is usually written as one word but there are exceptions as in the following:

| | | | |
|---|---|---|---|
| under-part | under-secretary | under-sexed | under-shrub |
| under-side | under-surface | | |

The following words do not need a hyphen:

| | | | |
|---|---|---|---|
| underachieve | underact | undercarriage | underclothes |
| undercoat | undercover | undercurrent | undercut |

| | | |
|---|---|---|
| underdeveloped | underdog | underemphasise |
| underemployed | underestimate | underexpose |
| underground | undergrowth | underhand |

## The prefix 'vice-'

When 'vice' is used to mean next in rank to a particular post, a hyphen is usually used:

| | | |
|---|---|---|
| vice-admiral | vice-chairman | vice-chamberlain |
| vice-captain | vice-chancellor | vice-president |

In the following words no hyphen is required:

viceregent (someone who exercises delegated power)
vicereine    viceroy

## ENDING WITH A SUFFIX

A suffix is a group of letters placed at the end of a word to qualify its meaning. In some cases a hyphen is placed before it to clarify the meaning. Below are some of the most common suffixes which require hyphens.

## The suffix '-all'

be-all    end-all

## The suffix '-away'

far-away    give-away    take-away

## The suffix '-back'

out-back    play-back    throw-back

## The suffix '-by'

lay-by    stand-by

## The suffix '-down'

| | | |
|---|---|---|
| back-down | broken-down | close-down |
| crack-down | put-down | run-down |
| show-down | shut-down | sit-down |

## The suffix '-in'

| | | | | |
|---|---|---|---|---|
| built-in | check-in | drive-in | phone-in | run-in |
| stand-in | trade-in | | | |

## The suffix '-less'

The suffix '-less' suggests 'without' the root word:

| | | | |
|---|---|---|---|
| doubt | doubtless | guilt | guiltless |
| home | homeless | joy | joyless |
| life | lifeless | number | numberless |
| power | powerless | relent | relentless |
| shame | shameless | tire | tireless |

## The suffix '-ness'

The suffix '-ness' is usually added to an adjective to make an **abstract noun**. Remember that the 'y' at the end of the adjective has to be changed into an 'i'. Remember also that if the root word ends in 'n', this letter will be doubled.

| Adjective | Noun | Adjective | Noun |
|---|---|---|---|
| bright | brightness | dark | darkness |
| empty | emptiness | great | greatness |
| happy | happiness | kind | kindness |
| lazy | laziness | lean | leanness |
| sore | soreness | still | stillness |
| ugly | ugliness | weak | weakness |

## The suffix '-off'

| | | | | | |
|---|---|---|---|---|---|
| brush-off | bully-off | cut-off | kick-off | lay-off | lift-off |
| pay-off | play-off | rip-off | show-off | take-off | tip-off |
| turn-off | well-off | write-off | | | |

## The suffix '-on'

| | | | |
|---|---|---|---|
| follow-on | hanger-on | head-on | knock-on |
| roll-on | try-on | turn-on | walk-on |

## The suffix '-out'

| | | | |
|---|---|---|---|
| black-out | check-out | cut-out | fall-out |
| hand-out | hide-out | knock-out | look-out |
| share-out | shoot-out | throw-out | try-out |
| wash-out | way-out | wipe-out | |

### The suffix '-over'

change-over           take-over           walk-over

### The suffix '-up'

| | | | | | |
|---|---|---|---|---|---|
| brush-up | build-up | call-up | clean-up | close-up | cover-up |
| fry-up | hang-up | hold-up | line-up | link-up | lock-up |
| make-up | pile-up | pin-up | press-ups | set-up | slap-up |
| slip-up | smash-up | stand-up | toss-up | warm-up | wind-up |
| write-up | | | | | |

Other suffixes that do not need hyphens will be dealt with later.

## HYPHENATING COMPOUND WORDS

A hyphen is usually used if two words are placed together to create a new word. Here are some of the combinations:

- two nouns (naming words)
- two adjectives (describing words)
- two verbs (doing words)
- a noun joined to an adjective.

### Joining two nouns

The following nouns require a hyphen to join the two words together:

| | | | |
|---|---|---|---|
| baby-sitter | baby-walker | back-door | belly-flop |
| blood-guilt | blood-money | book-ends | book-rest |
| bench-mark | catch-phrase | chair-lift | coal-box |
| coal-bunker | coal-cellar | corner-stone | duck-boards |
| dust-sheet | eye-shade | folk-dance | joy-ride |
| notice-board | price-list | rose-bud | rose-bush |
| scrum-half | sky-dive | time-scale | |

Note that bookmark is one word and does not have a hyphen.

### Joining two adjectives

Two adjectives may also be joined together with a hyphen:

| | | | |
|---|---|---|---|
| blue-eyed | cold-blooded | deep-rooted | long-sighted |
| right-handed | middle-aged | old-fashioned | short-sighted |

## Joining two verbs

Sometimes two verbs linked together heighten the meaning:

| | | | |
|---|---|---|---|
| crash-land | drip-dry | dry-clean | force-feed |
| hang-glide | test-drive | | |

## Joining a noun to an adjective

The following nouns are combined with an adjective:

| | | | |
|---|---|---|---|
| back-bencher | cut-price | half-back | loose-leaf |
| open-air | | | |

A colour may be qualified by the use of a noun attached to it although some of these are very well used:

| | | | |
|---|---|---|---|
| blood-red | rose-red | coal-black | sky-blue |
| snow-white | | | |

You may wish to create some original adjectives:

| | | |
|---|---|---|
| mould-green | leaf-brown | slush-grey |

## Joining a noun to a verb

The form of a verb varies according to the **tense**. Sometimes the **participles** of the verb can be added to a noun to form a new word. The **present participle** ends in '-ing' and the **past participle** usually ends in '-ed' although there are many exceptions.

*Adding the present participle*

The nouns in this case are linked to the present participle of the verb to make a new word:

| | | |
|---|---|---|
| back-breaking | blood-letting | joy-riding |
| much-raking | cheese-paring | filling-station |
| nerve-racking | | |

*Adding the past participle*

The past participle is added to the noun to create a new word:

| | | |
|---|---|---|
| bow-legged | grant-aided | hand-picked |

## Using a preposition

Sometimes there are more than two words linked by hyphens and in these cases a preposition is used. This is a word which indicates the position of one word to another. Look at the following examples:

| | | |
|---|---|---|
| down-to-earth | lady-in-waiting | brother-in-law |
| man-of-war | matter-of-fact | mother-in-law |
| out-of-date | right-of-way | sister-in-law |
| stick-in-the-mud | | |

## Using fractions and compound numbers

You should use a hyphen when writing fractions.

| | | |
|---|---|---|
| three-quarters | four-tenths | five-eighths |
| twenty-one | thirty-two | forty-three |
| fifty-four | sixty-five | seventy-six |
| eighty-seven | ninety-eight | ninety-nine |

## Combining French words

Some French words which have passed into our language are hyphenated:

| | | | |
|---|---|---|---|
| avant-garde | bric-a-brac | cul-de-sac | eau-de-cologne |
| mange-tout | pied-à-terre | sang-froid | vol-au-vent |

## CHECKLIST

- A prefix is placed *in front of* a word to qualify its meaning.

- A suffix appears at the *end* of a word.

- A hyphen links two words together.

- A hyphenated word may be:
  two nouns
  two adjectives
  two verbs
  noun and adjective.

- Use hyphens for fractions and compound numbers.

## PRACTISING WHAT YOU'VE LEARNT

1. What do the following prefixes mean?

   ante      anti      extra      far      neo

2. In the following sentences which words need hyphens?
   a. The subeditor reappeared waving the manuscript which was dotted with semicolons.
   b. When she reentered, she was accompanied by the vicechairman.
   c. The viceadmiral criticised the undersecretary for his underhand behaviour.
   d. She could not reach the checkout because of the blackout.
   e. The accident produced a knockon effect and Jane's car was a writeoff.

3. Add prefixes to the following words:

   | | | | |
   |---|---|---|---|
   | abridged | act | adorned | appear |
   | appoint | arm | attached | broken |
   | clean | colon | conscious | create |
   | crowned | final | hooked | laced |
   | marine | please | title | way |

4. Add suffixes to the following words:

   | | | | | |
   |---|---|---|---|---|
   | adorn | attach | beauty | doubt | happy |
   | hate | pain | pity | power | rest |

# 5

## Sorting Out the Changes

If a prefix or suffix is added to a root word, the word itself may in some cases have to be modified.

### ADDING TO THE ROOT WORD

If two words are combined to create a **compound word**, you may have to drop some letters. If the prefix ends in a double 'l', remove one 'l' before completing the word:

| | | | |
|------|----------|------|----------|
| all  | already  | all  | almost   |
| all  | also     | all  | although |
| all  | always   | full | fulfil   |
| skill| skilful  | well | welcome  |
| well | welfare  |      |          |

### USING '-FUL' OR '-FULL'

The word 'full' when written alone is always spelt with two 'ls'. When it is added to a noun or a verb to make the word into an adjective, only one 'l' is used as in the following:

| | | | |
|--------|-----------|---------|------------|
| beauty | beautiful | boast   | boastful   |
| care   | careful   | duty    | dutiful    |
| help   | helpful   | hope    | hopeful    |
| faith  | faithful  | fancy   | fanciful   |
| forget | forgetful | grace   | graceful   |
| hate   | hateful   | hope    | hopeful    |
| joy    | joyful    | truth   | truthful   |
| pain   | painful   | pity    | pitiful    |
| plenty | plentiful | rest    | restful    |
| tear   | tearful   | truth   | truthful   |
| spite  | spiteful  | success | successful |
| master | masterful | mercy   | merciful   |

| mourn | mournful | use | useful |
|-------|----------|-----|--------|
| waste | wasteful | wonder | wonderful |

Sometimes 'ful' is added to a noun to create another noun:

| bag | bagful | cup | cupful |
|-----|--------|-----|--------|
| fist | fistful | hand | handful |
| plate | plateful | mouth | mouthful |
| sack | sackful | spoon | spoonful |

## ENDING WITH '-LY'

'-ly' is usually added to adjectives to make an **adverb** which qualifies a verb. If the root word ends in 'l', don't forget to leave the 'l' and add 'ly' so you have a double 'l'. This can also apply to words ending in 'ful':

| actual | actually | beautiful | beautifully |
|--------|----------|-----------|-------------|
| careful | carefully | cruel | cruelly |
| faithful | faithfully | fatal | fatally |
| final | finally | formal | formally |
| general | generally | gradual | gradually |
| occasional | occasionally | personal | personally |
| real | really | special | specially |
| total | totally | usual | usually |

If the word ends in a consonant, there is also no change to the word before adding '-ly':

| bad | badly | bright | brightly |
|-----|-------|--------|----------|
| cold | coldly | correct | correctly |
| frequent | frequently | glad | gladly |
| humorous | humorously | imperious | imperiously |
| inept | ineptly | jubilant | jubilantly |
| vivid | vividly | | |

## Keeping the 'e'

If there is an 'e' at the end of a word, it is usually retained before adding 'ly'. It is a common mistake either to omit it or to put it before the 'y'; this is particularly the case in some words, so remember this rule:

| | | | |
|---|---|---|---|
| complete | completely | definite | definitely |
| desperate | desperately | fortunate | fortunately |
| grave | gravely | immediate | immediately |
| love | lovely | separate | separately |
| sincere | sincerely | | |

## Changing the 'e'

If a word ends in 'le', the 'l' is retained and the 'e' replaced by 'y':

| | | | |
|---|---|---|---|
| bubble | bubbly | capable | capably |
| despicable | despicably | double | doubly |
| gentle | gently | humble | humbly |
| incredible | incredibly | knowlegeable | knowledgeably |
| possible | possibly | probable | probably |
| remarkable | remarkably | single | singly |
| terrible | terribly | | |

## Changing the 'y'

If the word ends in 'y', in most cases the 'y' is changed into an 'i' before adding '-ly':

| | | | |
|---|---|---|---|
| busy | busily | crazy | crazily |
| extraordinary | extraordinarily | hazy | hazily |
| healthy | healthily | heavy | heavily |
| hungry | hungrily | merry | merrily |
| necessary | necessarily | shabby | shabbily |

## Looking at exceptions

As with many rules, there are exceptions to the above.

The adjective 'coy' ends with 'y' but this is not changed before adding 'ly': coyly.

'Day' and 'gay' end in 'y' and, as in the earlier examples, the 'y' is changed to an 'i' although there is only one syllable (a single unit of sound): daily, gaily.

If the word already ends in a double 'l', you need only add a 'y':

| | | |
|---|---|---|
| dull | dully | full | fully |

'Due', 'true' and 'whole' all end in 'e' so remove this before adding 'ly':

| due | duly | | true | truly |
|-----|------|--|------|-------|
| whole | wholly | | | |

*Using 'friendly'*

The word 'friendly' is an adjective and describes a noun although it is now sometimes used incorrectly as an adverb. To form the adverb 'ly' has to be added to the adjective 'friendly' and the 'y' changed to an 'i' to produce the word 'friendlily'. It is a clumsy word and it is often better to reword your sentence to avoid using it. Look at the following examples:

– She behaved *friendlily* towards me.
– She behaved in a *friendly manner* towards me.

The adverb in the first sentence is awkward. It is better to use the adjective in the second one. 'Manner' is an abstract noun.

### Looking at words ending in '-ic'

If a word ends in '-ic', it is usually necessary to add '-ally' instead of just '-ly':

| | | | |
|--|--|--|--|
| automatic | automatically | basic | basically |
| characteristic | characteristically | comic | comically |
| critic | critically | drastic | drastically |
| enthusiastic | enthusiastically | frantic | frantically |
| heroic | heroically | pathetic | pathetically |
| rhythmic | rhythmically | scientific | scientifically |
| specific | specifically | stoic | stoically |
| tragic | tragically | music | musically |
| mechanic | mechanically | | |

### DOUBLING THE CONSONANT

If a word ends in a single consonant and you wish to add a suffix beginning with a vowel, you will usually need to double the consonant before adding it if there is only one syllable or if the stress falls on the last syllable.

| | | |
|--|--|--|
| annul | annulled | annulling |
| bat | batted | batting |
| bit | bitter | bitten |
| cancel | cancelled | cancelling |

| | | |
|---|---|---|
| compel | compelled | compelling |
| counsel | counselled | counselling |
| drop | dropped | dropping |
| enrol | enrolled | enrolling |
| hop | hopped | hopping |
| intial | initialled | initialling |
| label | labelled | labelling |
| libel | libelled | libelling |
| propel | propelled | propelling |

## Looking at the exceptions

Where the stress in a multi-syllable word does not fall on the last syllable, it is not usually necessary to double the consonant:

| | | |
|---|---|---|
| benefit | benefited | benefiting |
| bias | biased | biasing |
| blanket | blanketed | blanketing |
| carpet | carpeted | carpeting |
| cricket | cricketer | cricketing |
| docket | docketed | docketing |
| fillet | filleted | filleting |
| focus | focused | focusing |
| gallop | galloped | galloping |
| market | marketed | marketing |
| offer | offered | offering |
| picket | picketed | picketing |
| target | targeted | targeting |

Some consonants are *not* doubled before adding a suffix beginning with a vowel. These are: w, x and y:

| | | |
|---|---|---|
| cox | coxed | coxing |
| cloy | cloyed | cloying |
| fray | frayed | fraying |
| stay | stayed | staying |
| tax | taxed | taxing |
| tow | towed | towing |
| toy | toyed | toying |
| vex | vexed | vexing |

If the consonant is preceded by two vowels, it is not doubled when adding a suffix beginning with a vowel:

| beat  | beaten  | beating  |
|-------|---------|----------|
| break |         | breaking |
| creak | creaked | creaking |
| creep |         | creeping |
| droop | drooped | drooping |
| fail  | failed  | failing  |
| flail | flailed | flailing |
| greet | greeted | greeting |
| group | grouped | grouping |
| hail  | hailed  | hailing  |
| heap  | heaped  | heaping  |
| hoot  | hooted  | hooting  |
| sail  | sailed  | sailing  |
| seat  | seated  | seating  |
| soar  | soared  | soaring  |
| sleep |         | sleeping |
| trail | trailed | trailing |
| treat | treated | treating |

If the root word ends with two consonants, it is obviously unnecessary to double the last one before adding the suffix.

| bang   | banged   | banging   |
|--------|----------|-----------|
| clock  | clocked  | clocking  |
| crash  | crashed  | crashing  |
| dash   | dashed   | dashing   |
| fast   | fasted   | fasting   |
| fault  | faulted  | faulting  |
| fight  |          | fighting  |
| light  | lighted  | lighting  |
| lack   | lacked   | lacking   |
| lurch  | lurched  | lurching  |
| prick  | pricked  | pricking  |
| sack   | sacked   | sacking   |
| search | searched | searching |
| sight  | sighted  | sighting  |
| track  | tracked  | tracking  |
| turn   | turned   | turning   |

## Adding a suffix starting with a consonant

A suffix starting with a consonant usually changes the meaning of the word and converts it into a different part of speech. In most cases you can leave the root word as it is and just add the suffix:

| | | | |
|---|---|---|---|
| annul | annulment | allot | allotment |
| abridge | abridgement | advertise | advertisement |
| amaze | amazement | bitter | bitterness |
| brother | brotherhood | child | childhood |
| commit | commitment | companion | companionship |
| court | courtship | coy | coyness |
| doubt | doubtless | duke | dukedom |
| earl | earldom | false | falsehood |
| fellow | fellowship | free | freedom |
| friend | friendship | hard | hardship |
| odd | oddment | member | membership |
| official | officialdom | power | powerless |
| scholar | scholarship | sister | sisterhood |

## COPING WITH THE 'E'

Many words end with a silent 'e' and in single syllable words the preceding vowel is usually a 'long' one. When adding a suffix beginning with a vowel, it is usually necessary to remove the 'e':

| | | | |
|---|---|---|---|
| bite | biting | brake | braking |
| date | dating | dupe | duping |
| flake | flaking | flame | flaming |
| grate | grating | grope | groping |
| hate | hating | hike | hiking |
| hope | hoping | tape | taping |

### Looking at the exceptions

When a word ends in a 'soft' 'g' sound instead of a 'hard' one, the 'e' is retained as in the following:

| | | | |
|---|---|---|---|
| age | ageing | courage | courageous |
| singe | singeing | | |

Occasionally the 'e' at the end of a word is pronounced as an extra syllable:

| | | | |
|---|---|---|---|
| anemone | apostrophe | catastrophe | simile |

## CHANGING THE TENSE

Verbs ('doing' or 'being' words) can be used in the past, present or future and are often added suffixes to change the tense. To change a 'doing' verb from the present to the past, it is usually necessary to add 'd' or 'ed' to the end. Remember that you may have to double the consonant at the end.

| Present | Past | Past participle |
| --- | --- | --- |
| I dance | I danced | (have) danced |
| you play | you played | (have) played |
| he travels | he travelled | (has) travelled |
| she criticises | she criticised | (has) criticised |
| it chases | it chased | (has) chased |
| we plan | we planned | (have) planned |
| they move | they moved | (have) moved |

Notice that in the above examples, the past participle is the same word as the past tense. This is not so in all cases.

### Looking at the exceptions

The verb 'to be' changes the word in the past tense (refer to Chapter 3). Some 'doing' words also change the word instead of adding 'ed' and the past participle is sometimes different again. Look at the following examples:

| Present | Past | Past participle |
| --- | --- | --- |
| bleed | bled | bled |
| blow | blew | blown |
| break | broke | broken |
| catch | caught | caught |
| choose | chose | chosen |
| do | did | done |
| draw | drew | drawn |
| drive | drove | driven |
| eat | ate | eaten |
| fall | fell | fallen |
| fight | fought | fought |
| find | found | found |
| light | lit | lit |
| ride | rode | ridden |
| rise | rose | risen |

| | | |
|---|---|---|
| see | saw | seen |
| shake | shook | shaken |
| shine | shone | shone |
| sit | sat | sat |
| speak | spoke | spoken |
| spend | spent | spent |
| steal | stole | stolen |
| strive | strove | striven |
| swear | swore | sworn |
| take | took | taken |
| teach | taught | taught |
| tell | told | told |
| think | thought | thought |
| throw | threw | thrown |
| wear | wore | worn |
| win | won | won |
| wind | wound | wound |
| write | wrote | written |

*Keeping the same word*

The verbs 'to read' and 'to beat' retain the same word for both present and the past tenses but 'read' (present tense) is pronounced with a long 'ee' sound while the past tense is a short 'e' as in 'red'.

## Changing the vowels

In the following verbs the 'a' in the past tense is changed to 'u' for the past participle:

| *Present* | *Past* | *Past participle* |
|---|---|---|
| begin | began | begun |
| drink | drank | drunk |
| run | ran | run |
| shrink | shrank | shrunk |
| spring | sprang | sprung |
| stink | stank | stunk |
| swim | swam | swum |

*Using 't' instead of 'ed'*

The following verbs use 't' instead of 'ed' to form the past tense and the past participle:

| Present | Past | Past participle |
|---------|------|-----------------|
| build | built | built |
| burn | burnt | burnt |
| creep | crept | crept |
| deal | dealt | dealt |
| feel | felt | felt |
| learn | learnt | learnt |
| lean | leant | leant |
| sleep | slept | slept |
| sweep | swept | swept |
| weep | wept | wept |

## LOOKING AT ENDINGS

The endings of some words are confusing and you may not know which is the correct one to use. Unfortunately there are few rules to help you so the words have to be learnt or you will have to use a dictionary.

### Is it '-able' or '-ible'?
The endings '-able' and '-ible' usually form adjectives. It may help you to find the correct ending if you think of the noun that relates to the adjective. If the last syllable contains an 'a' towards the end, the word will usually end in '-able'. Similarly if there is an 'i', the ending is likely to be '-ible'.

| Noun | Adjective | Noun | Adjective |
|------|-----------|------|-----------|
| adoration | adorable | accession | accessible |
| admiration | admirable | admission | admissible |
| abomination | abominable | comprehension | comprehensible |
| inflation | inflatable | digestion | digestible |
| irritation | irritable | division | divisible |

*Other words with '-able' endings*

| | | | |
|------|------|------|------|
| acceptable | adaptable | arguable | available |
| comfortable | considerable | inflammable | laughable |
| objectionable | perishable | pleasurable | regrettable |
| tolerable | undeniable | unmistakable | variable |

### Other words with '-ible' endings

| | | | |
|---|---|---|---|
| admissible | xaudible | collapsible | combustible |
| compatible | contemptible | convertible | corruptible |
| credible | edible | fallible | flexible |
| feasible | incomprehensible | indelible | infallible |
| intangible | invincible | legible | permissible |

### Exceptions

Some words retain the 'e' before adding '-able'. This is so if there is a soft 'c' or 'g' at the end of the root word:

| | | | |
|---|---|---|---|
| notice | noticeable | peace | peaceable |
| pronounce | pronounceable | service | serviceable |
| trace | traceable | replace | replaceable |
| bridge | bridgeable | charge | chargeable |
| change | changeable | knowledge | knowledgeable |
| marriage | marriageable | | |

### Other exceptions

Other words that keep the 'e' before '-able' are:

| | | | |
|---|---|---|---|
| blame | blameable | give | giveable |
| like | likeable | name | nameable |
| rate | rateable | sale | saleable |
| share | shareable | size | sizeable |
| shake | shakeable | tame | tameable |

Note that if '-ing' is added to some of the above words the 'e' is removed:

| | | | | |
|---|---|---|---|---|
| blaming | giving | liking | naming | rating |
| sharing | sizing | shaking | taming | timing |

### Is it '-ce' or '-se-?

In most cases the noun ends in '-ce' and the verb ends in '-se'.

| Noun | Verb |
|---|---|
| advice | advise |
| device | devise |
| licence | license |

The following words end with 'y' instead of 'e' and both are pronounced as an extra syllable:

*noun*: prophecy (ee sound)    *verb*: prophesy (long 'i' sound)

## Is it 'a' or 'e'?

It is not always easy to decide whether an 'a' or an 'e' introduces the suffix. There are, unfortunately, no rules to help you so the words have to be learnt.

*Some adjectives ending in '-ant'*

| | | | |
|---|---|---|---|
| abundant | adamant | arrogant | blatant |
| buoyant | constant | distant | dominant |
| elegant | extravagant | exuberant | flagrant |
| poignant | pregnant | redundant | repentant |
| relevant | reluctant | repugnant | resonant |
| significant | vacant | vibrant | |

*Some nouns ending in '-ant'*

| | | | |
|---|---|---|---|
| assistant | celebrant | claimant | deodorant |
| dependant | descendant | emigrant | militant |
| peasant | pendant | pheasant | tenant |
| transplant | truant | tyrant | vagrant |

*Some adjectives ending in '-ent'*

| | | | |
|---|---|---|---|
| absent | apparent | ardent | belligerent |
| coherent | consistent | decadent | dependent |
| effluent | diligent | eminent | evident |
| expedient | fluorescent | frequent | independent |
| obedient | reminiscent | | |

*Some nouns ending in '-ent'*

| | | | |
|---|---|---|---|
| ascent | content | convent | delinquent |
| equivalent | extent | incumbent | patient |
| portent | president | recipient | superintendent |
| tangent | | | |

## Is it '-ance' or '-ence'?

Nouns often use the above suffix. If applicable the 'a' or 'e' will follow the same pattern as the previous examples.

*Nouns ending in '-ance'*

| | | | |
|---|---|---|---|
| abundance | arrogance | appearance | assonance |
| assurance | defiance | distance | disturbance |
| elegance | entrance | extravagance | grievance |
| insurance | performance | perseverance | resistance |
| resonance | semblance | surveillance | temperance |

*Nouns ending in '-ence'*

| | | | |
|---|---|---|---|
| absence | commence | consequence | correspondence |
| eminence | essence | evidence | excellence |
| expedience | impudence | presence | pretence |
| reminiscence | reverence | sentence | sequence |

## Using 's' or 'z'

There is often confusion as to whether words should end with '-ise' or '-ize'. If the 'i' is pronounced with either a short vowel sound as in 'lip' or a long 'e' sound as in 'see', the ending is usually '-ise':

premise    promise    expertise    reprise

The problem often arises with words which end with a 'long' 'i' sound. The following words always take the 's' ending.

*Verbs*

| | | | | |
|---|---|---|---|---|
| advertise | apprise | arise | chastise | circumcise |
| devise | emphasise | franchise | improvise | revise |

*Nouns*

demise    enterprise    merchandise

The following words can be both nouns and verbs:

compromise    disguise    exercise (can also be an adjective)
surprise

The following words have traditionally been spelt with an '-ize' ending but the alternative '-ise' is now acceptable and is becoming increasingly popular:

| | | |
|---|---|---|
| agonize (-ise) | appetizer (-iser) | civilize (-ise) |
| colonize (-ise) | criticize (-ise) | fertilizer (-iser) |
| legalize (-ise) | recognize (-ise) | standardize (-ise) |

Note the following words:

| | | | |
|---|---|---|---|
| apprise (verb) | to inform | apprize (verb) | to value |
| prise (verb) | to open | prize (noun) | a reward |

### Ending with '-le'

If two consonants follow a short vowel sound, the ending is usually '-le':

| | | | | | |
|---|---|---|---|---|---|
| angle | battle | bramble | bristle | brittle | cattle |
| crumple | cuddle | dazzle | fiddle | handle | humble |
| hurtle | mantle | middle | muscle | nestle | nettle |
| nimble | paddle | prattle | raffle | rattle | riddle |
| ruffle | saddle | simple | single | thimble | thistle |
| twiddle | wrestle | wriggle | | | |

Words whose root ends in 'c' or 'k' also usually take the '-le' ending:

| | | | | | |
|---|---|---|---|---|---|
| ankle | article | barnacle | buckle | bicycle | castle |
| chuckle | crackle | fickle | icicle | miracle | obstacle |
| rankle | sparkle | spectacle | sprinkle | suckle | twinkle |
| uncle | vehicle | winkle | wrinkle | | |

Other words which have an '-le' ending are:

| | | | | | |
|---|---|---|---|---|---|
| beetle | beadle | bible | bridle | girdle | liable |
| needle | stable | table | | | |

### Other endings

Other words might end with '-el' '-il' or '-ol' but unfortunately there is no rule to help you to decide on the correct ending. However the following letters are *never* followed by '-le': m, n, v, w.

The spelling of the following words may have to be learnt:

| | | | | | |
|---|---|---|---|---|---|
| angel | camel | cannibal | chisel | crystal | hospital |
| hotel | label | marvel | model | novel | original |
| parallel | pedal | peril | petal | pistol | pupil |
| rascal | royal | sandal | tunnel | usual | visual |
| vowel | | | | | |

## Ending words with '-ous'

A number of words end in '-ous' and many are preceded by a consonant. They are usually adjectives:

| | | |
|---|---|---|
| ambidextrous | anonymous | blasphemous |
| callous | credulous | dangerous |
| enormous | fabulous | famous |
| garrulous | grievous | humorous |
| infamous | jealous | marvellous |
| murderous | nervous | perilous |
| preposterous | rapturous | ridiculous |
| scurrilous | solicitous | sonorous |
| treacherous | | |

Some words have an 'i' before the '-ous' and the following words are pronounced with a 'sh' sound:

| | | | |
|---|---|---|---|
| anxious | atrocious | conscious | ferocious |
| gracious | luscious | obnoxious | precious |
| spacious | superstitious | suspicious | tenacious |
| voracious | vicious | | |

In other cases the 'i' is pronounded as 'ee' thus creating another syllable:

| | | | |
|---|---|---|---|
| curious | delirious | fastidious | furious |
| glorious | hilarious | illustrious | impervious |
| luxurious | previous | salubrious | sanctimonious |
| serious | spacious | supercilious | various |
| vicarious | victorious | | |

There are also words which have an 'e' before the '-ous' and in this case the vowel is pronounced as 'ee':

| | | | |
|---|---|---|---|
| beauteous | bounteous | courteous | erroneous |
| hideous | miscellaneous | nauseous | piteous |
| simultaneous | spontaneous | | |

In the following words the 'e' or the 'i' is retained because the 'g' is soft:

| | | | |
|---|---|---|---|
| advantageous | courageous | gorgeous | outrageous |
| contagious | religious | sacrilegious | |

## Ending with '-ion'
Words ending with '-ion' are invariably nouns and whatever the preceding consonant the suffix is usually pronounced 'sh'.

*Words ending in '-tion'*

| | | | |
|---|---|---|---|
| action | addiction | administration | attention |
| civilisation | communication | competition | conception |
| condition | description | diction | education |
| fraction | generation | genuflection | graduation |
| identification | imagination | induction | installation |
| matriculation | motion | nation | obstruction |
| occupation | partition | personification | prescription |
| position | promotion | pronunciation | punctuation |
| radiation | reception | rejection | remuneration |
| restitution | resurrection | revolution | sanction |
| solution | station | suggestion | termination |
| transportation | transcription | translation | tribulation |
| vacation | vaccination | veneration | vocation |

*Words ending with '-sion'*
There are fewer words ending with '-sion':

| | | | |
|---|---|---|---|
| collision | comprehension | condescension | derision |
| mansion | mission | pension | permission |
| persuasion | profusion | suspension | transfusion |

*Words ending with '-xion'*
A few words end with '-xion' but some may also use 'ct' instead of 'x':

| | | |
|---|---|---|
| crucifixion | deflexion (deflection) | fluxion |
| genuflexion (genuflection) | inflexion (inflection) | |

## Ending with '-ian'
Some words end with 'ian' and the preceding consonant is usually a 'c' and it is pronounced 'sh'. These are usually job titles.

*Words ending '-cian'*

| | | | |
|---|---|---|---|
| beautician | electrician | magician | mathematician |
| musician | optician | paediatrician | politician |
| statistician | technician | | |

## CHECKLIST

- Retain the 'e' at the end of word before adding 'ly'.

- Change the 'y' into an 'i' before adding 'ly'.

- Add 'ally' after 'ic'.

- Apart from w, x and y, double the consonant before adding a suffix unless two vowels precede it.

- Remove the 'e' at the end when adding a suffix beginning with a vowel.

## PRACTISING WHAT YOU'VE LEARNT

Correct the spelling mistakes in the following passage:

She was so *beautifull* that he was *allmost* in love with her. He knew she was a *dutyful* daughter but he was *hopefull* that she would *finaly* agree to go out with him. He knew she *usualy* walked in the park in the morning. When she appeared, he *immediatly* went towards her and asked if he could join her. She shook her head *gentley* and went on her way. He was *terribley* hurt but realised that she would not *automaticly* become his friend. His brain was racing *franticly* as he *planed* his next move and *hopped* she would speak to him.

# 6

## Avoiding Common Mistakes

Because English spelling is complicated, there are many common mistakes to avoid. To make life more difficult some words with different meanings are pronounced in the same way but spelt differently. It is necessary to learn the ones that cause you problems.

### SORTING OUT PROBLEM WORDS

Words that are pronounced the same but spelt differently are called **homonyms** or **homophones**.

### Dealing with homonyms

Homonyms have to be learnt. There are rarely rules to help you with the correct spelling:

| | | | |
|---|---|---|---|
| air | gaseous substance | heir | successor |
| aisle | passage between seats | isle | land surrounded by water |
| allowed | permitted | aloud | audible |
| altar | table at end of church | alter | change |
| bare | naked | bear | an animal |
| bark | sound dog makes covering of tree trunk | barque | sailing ship |
| bean | a vegetable | been | past tense of the verb 'to be' |
| be | verb | bee | insect |
| beech | a tree | beach | sand or shingle beside sea |
| beer | an alcoholic drink | bier | wooden plank bearing corpse |
| bite | to use teeth | byte | a computer term |
| blew | past tense of 'blow' | blue | a colour |
| board | *noun*: piece of timber *verb*: to lodge | bored | finding something dull |
| boy | a young male | buoy | marker in sea for ships |

| | | | |
|---|---|---|---|
| bow | to bend head | bough | branch of tree |
| bread | food made from flour | bred | past tense of breed |
| by | at side of something | buy | purchase |
| | | bye | a run in cricket awarded by umpire |
| caught | past tense of catch | court | space enclosed by buildings |
| cent | monetary unit | sent | past tense of send |
| | | scent | perfume |
| check | sudden stop to inspect | cheque | written order to bank to pay money |
| council | an administrative body | counsel | to give advice |
| current | water or air moving in a particular direction | currant | dried fruit |
| ewe | female sheep | yew | a tree |
| | | you | second person pronoun |
| dear | loved; expensive | deer | animal |
| faint | become unconscious | feint | to make a diversionary move |
| fare | money charged for journey | fair | opposite to dark beautiful gathering of people for trade and entertainment |
| feat | notable achievement | feet | plural of foot measurement |
| fir | a tree | fur | an animal's covering |
| grate | *noun*: metal frame for fuel *verb*: produce small pieces by rubbing against something | great | huge; famous |
| herd | a group of cattle | heard | past tense of hear |
| here | in this place | hear | to be aware of sound |
| hole | a cavity | whole | something complete |
| idle | lazy | idol | object of worship |
| know | to have knowledge | no | opposite of yes |
| passed | past tense of pass | past | time gone by to pass by |
| peace | freedom from war | piece | a portion |
| peal | a ring of bells | peel | rind of fruit |
| place | particular area | plaice | a fish |

| | | | |
|---|---|---|---|
| poor | opposite to rich | pore | tiny opening in skin |
| | | pour | tip liquid out of container |
| quay | landing place for ships | key | implement for locking |
| rain | water from clouds | reign | monarch's rule |
| | | rein | lead for controlling horse |
| read | understand written words | reed | grass-like plant |
| right | correct | rite | religious ceremony |
| wright | craftsman | write | put words on paper |
| road | highway | rode | past tense of ride |
| root | part of plant in soil | route | course followed to a destination |
| rough | not gentle | ruff | frilly collar worn in sixteenth century |
| sail | sheet of material on a ship to travel on water | sale | noun from the verb to sell |
| sea | expanse of salt water | see | to have sight of |
| seam | place where two pieces of material are joined | seem | to appear to be |
| sew | stitches made by needle and thread | sow | to plant seeds |
| | | so | indicating extent of something |
| sole | fish underneath of foot | soul | spirit |
| some | a particular group | sum | the total |
| son | male offspring | sun | source of light |
| stake | wooden stave | steak | cooked meat |
| suite | furniture piece of music | sweet | confectionery dessert |
| tail | end of animal | tale | story |
| tare | a type of corn weed | tear | to rip |
| taught | past tense of teach | taut | tight |
| team | group working together | teem | overflowing with |
| tear | salt water from eyes | tier | rows placed above each other |
| thyme | a herb | time | duration |

| | | | |
|---|---|---|---|
| threw | hurled | through | pass into one side and out of the other |
| tire | to become weary | tyre | rubber covering on a wheel |
| to | in direction of | too | as well or excessively |
| | | two | the number |
| vain | conceited | vein | vessel in body for carrying blood |
| | | vane | weathercock |
| waist | middle part of body | waste | rubbish or uncultivated land |
| weather | atmospheric conditions | whether | introduces an alternative |
| whine | high pitched sound | wine | alcoholic drink |
| wood | timber | would | past tense of will |

## Looking at other problem words

There are a number of other words which can cause problems because of their similarity in sound. Some of these are:

| | | | |
|---|---|---|---|
| accept | to receive | except | apart from |
| affect | to influence | effect | to bring about |
| bridal | adjective from bride | bridle | a horse's lead |
| canvas | thick material | canvass | to persuade voters |
| complement | to make complete | compliment | express admiration |
| desert | expanse of sand | dessert | pudding, sweet |
| ensure | to make sure | insure | to protect from loss |
| envelop | to cover something | envelope | wrapping for letter |
| formally | conventionally | formerly | previously |
| gorilla | an animal | guerrilla | fighter in small force |
| lightening | to make lighter | lightning | flash before thunder |
| loose | not restrained | lose | to mislay |
| lumbar | lower part of back | lumber | move awkwardly rubbish |
| persecute | to cause suffering | prosecute | to take to court |

| principal | head of a college | principle | rule or standard |
| stationary | to be still | stationery | paper and other goods |
| storey | floor of a building | story | tale |

## Confusing 'their', 'there' and 'they're'

'Their' is a possessive adjective and is placed before a noun to indicate ownership.

– *Their* books are on the table.

'There' is an adverb of place and shows *where* something is.

– *There* is my house.

'They're' is an abbreviation short for 'they are'. The apostrophe replaces the 'a'.

– *They're* moving today.

## Confusing 'were', 'where' and 'wear'

'Were' is the past tense of the verb 'to be'.

– They *were* a happy couple.

'Where' is an adverb of place.

– *Where* is my pen?

– This is the place *where* the battle started.

'Wear' is the past tense of the verb 'to wear'.

– I *wear* my poppy with pride.

## Making it easy

One way to avoid confusion in homonyms is to find, if possible, a link between words. The words ending in 'ere' usually denote place:

here        there        where

The figure two is often confused with to and too. If you think of the following words, you should remember there must be a 'w' in the number.

twice        twenty        twins

## Distinguishing between 'who's' and 'whose'

'Who's' is short for 'who is'.

– Who's that handsome man?

Do not confuse it with 'whose' which is usually linked to a noun.

– The girl, whose arm was broken, walked on to the platform.

## Shortening 'have'

In some cases 'have' can be shortened to ''ve' and because this sounds like 'of' another common mistake is to use 'of' instead of ''ve'. Try to avoid this error.

Could have = could've
Might have = might've
Would have = would've

## Shortening 'are'

'Are' can also be shortened by removing the 'a' when it is joined to another word.

You are = you're
They are = they're
We are = we're

## Joining words incorrectly

Small words are sometimes incorrectly joined together. Frequent mistakes are:

abit       alot       alright       incase       infront

These should be two words:

a bit       a lot       all right       in case       in front

## Using 'bought' or 'brought'

There is sometimes confusion as to whether the 'r' should be included in the above words
'Bought' is the past tense of the verb 'to buy'. There is no 'r'.
– I *bought* fresh bread yesterday.
'Brought' is the past tense of the verb 'to bring'. An 'r' *is* necessary.
– I *brought* my new dress for you to see.

## Using 'speak' and 'speech'

'Speak' is the verb and is spelt with 'ea'.
– I will *speak* to her.
'Speech' is the noun and is spelt with double 'e'.
– His *speech* was excellent.

**Deleting the 'u'**

When a suffix is added to a word ending in '-our', the 'u' is sometimes omitted:

glamour      glamorous        humour        humorous

*but*

colour       colourful

**Using the '-cede' suffix**

The suffix that sounds like 'seed' is usually spelt 'cede'.

precede      recede

*Exceptions*

The exceptions are:

*sede*:      supersede
*ceed*:      exceed        proceed          succeed

## LOOKING AT COMMONLY MISSPELT WORDS

There are a number of words that are frequently misspelt and many of these have to be learnt as there are often no rules to help you:

| | | | |
|---|---|---|---|
| absence | abysmal | acquaint | acquire |
| across | address | advertisement | aggravate |
| alleluia | annual | appearance | archaeology |
| arrangement | auxiliary | awkward | because |
| beginning | believe | beautiful | business |
| character | carcass | centre | cemetery |
| cellar | chameleon | choose | committee |
| computer | condemn | conscious | daily |
| definitely | description | desperate | develop |
| diarrhoea | difference | dining | disappear |
| disappoint | discipline | desperate | dissatisfied |
| doctor | doubt | eerie | eight |
| eighth | embarrass | empty | encyclopaedia |
| exaggerate | exceed | exercise | excitement |
| exhaust | exhibition | existence | familiar |
| February | fierce | first | foreigner |
| forty | fortunately | frightening | fulfil |

| | | | |
|---|---|---|---|
| government | glamorous | gradually | grammar |
| guard | haemorrhage | haemorrhoids | harass |
| height | honorary | humorous | idea |
| immediately | independence | island | jewellery |
| journey | khaki | knowledge | laboratory |
| lacquer | language | league | leisure |
| liaison | lonely | lovely | maintenance |
| massacre | metaphor | miniature | miscellaneous |
| mischievous | miserably | misspell | necessary |
| neighbour | neither | ninth | occasion |
| occur | occurred | occurrence | omit |
| opportunity | opposite | paid | paraffin |
| parallel | particularly | playwright | possess |
| precede | preparation | procedure | preferred |
| privilege | probably | profession | professor |
| pronunciation | pursue | questionnaire | queue |
| receipt | receive | recognise | restaurant |
| rhyme | rhythm | said | schedule |
| science | scissors | secretary | separate |
| sergeant | similar | simile | sincerely |
| skilful | spaghetti | strength | subtle |
| succeed | surprise | suppress | temporary |
| thief | though | tragedy | tried |
| truly | unnecessary | until | usage |
| usual | vacuum | vehicle | vigorous |
| vicious | Wednesday | weird | woollen |
| womb | yield | | |

## Sorting out the confusion

The following words are also often spelt incorrectly:

| | |
|---|---|
| Britain: | *not* Britian |
| brain: | an organ inside the skull |
| Brian: | a name |
| diary: | a book in which you keep a record of your life |
| dairy: | a place where milk is churned and made into butter and cheese |
| lightning: | this comes before thunder |
| lightening: | this means to lighten something – to make it lighter |
| lose: | verb: to mislay or fail to win |
| loose: | adjective: not held tightly by any bonds |

## Using mnemonic devices

A mnemonic device is an aid for improving your memory. The 'm' is silent. You could think up your own to help you to remember difficult spellings.

*Examples*
– I *hear* with my *ears*.
– I like having *tea* by the *sea*.
– A station*er* sells station*ery*.

## HOMING IN ON YOUR PROBLEM WORDS

There are probably words you frequently misspell. Most people, however accurate they are usually, have a 'mental block' about certain words. Researchers into spelling problems have dubbed these words FOMs – an acronym for **frequent occurrence misspelling**.

## Identifying your FOMs

Once you have identified your FOMs, you are on the way to improving your spelling. Write down on several large pieces of paper or card the correct spelling of six or seven of your FOMs. Then scatter them throughout the house. Prop up a card on your desk, use a magnet to attach it to your fridge, pin it on your notice board and hang it over your bed!

The constant awareness of your FOMs should help you to spell the words correctly when next you use them. However, if this doesn't work for you try to find a mnemonic device to help you. This can be as silly as you like; the sillier the better as you are more likely to remember it!

The combination of the lists and the mnemonic devices should improve your spelling. When you have mastered your first list of FOMs, follow the same pattern with another set. If you persevere, you will be amazed at the improvement in your spelling.

## USING A SPELL-CHECK

The **spell-check** on your computer is useful but it will only pick up incorrect spelling. It won't tell you whether you have used the correct word. You must check your work manually as well or you may end up with something like this!

– Thank yew for you're letter. Wood yew like too go two Cornwall for a weak when the whether improves?

You may also find that the spell-check occasionally differs from the dictionary. It will sometimes suggest a hyphen when the dictionary has one word. In case of doubt, always use the dictionary spelling.

## CHECKLIST

- A homonym is a word that is spelt differently but pronounced the same as another word.

- Don't confuse 'their', 'there' and 'they're'.

- The abbreviation for 'have' is ''ve' *not* 'of'.

- 'Brought' is from 'bring': 'bought' is from 'buy'.

- A spell-check will only *correct* words – not replace them.

## PRACTISING WHAT YOU'VE LEARNT

Correct the following passage:

Dick was not *aloud* to go to the *see*. He wanted to *sea* it but he had been *court* being *ruff* with a playmate. He was *board*. He tried to *right* his *dairy* but he was *lonley*. He wanted to *right* a *storey* but there was a flash of *lightening* and he had left his *stationary* inside.

The sky was no longer *blew* so he *immediatley* ran into the school. He *new* the *principle* would be angry with him. In his class room sat Jacques, the *foriegner*. He was doing some *grammer* exersises but he found *riting sentenses* difficult.

*Miserablely*, Dick sat down. He was not *suprised* that Jaques *mispelled* so many words. He pulled on his *woolen* mitts because his hands were cold.

# 7

# Using Apostrophes and Abbreviations

**Apostrophes** are used to show possession and also to replace letters if words are abbreviated.

## SHOWING POSSESSION

There are some rules you can learn which will help you to know where to put the apostrophe when it is used to show possession.

### Dealing with the singular

When a singular noun shows possession, an 's' is added and the apostrophe is placed *before* it. It must be followed by another noun although in some cases there may be an adjective before the noun:
– Jack's house was burnt down.
– The book's pages were torn.
– The girl's ball was lost.
– Her father's will was a surprise.
– The thief stole Lucy's valuable necklace.
– All the old lady's treasured possessions were placed in a bag.

   Apostrophes are also required in the following cases:
– She was given a week's leave.
– The Smiths had a month's holiday.
– He felt exhausted after his day's work.
– There would be a year's delay before her book was published.
– Yesterday's storm caused much damage.
– Tomorrow's weather forecast is good.
– Today's matches were cancelled.
– Her term's work was wasted.

   If there are two nouns which share the possession you need only put an apostrophe in the second one.
– Jo and Sarah's examination results were good.
– Peter and Clive's footwork helped to win the match.

An apostrophe should also be used in the following:
- She has an appointment at the hairdresser's. (Salon' is 'understood'.)
- I must buy a paper at the newsagent's. ('Shop' is 'understood'.)
- She always buys her meat from the butcher's. ('Shop' is 'understood'.)

If a noun showing possession ends in a single 's', in most cases you have a choice. You may add the apostrophe alone after the word or you may add the extra 's' as well.
- King James' (s) comments on tobaco are still remembered.
- Charles' (s) dog had died.
- King Louis' (s) new palace was magnificent. (In this case it is probably better to omit the 's'.)
If the noun ends in double 's', it is necessary to add the extra 's' for ease of pronunciation.
- The princess's funeral service was very moving.
- The class's behaviour was disgraceful.
- The duchess's ball gown was beautiful.
- The witness's testimony caused uproar in the court.

## Dealing with the plural
Most nouns add an 's' to make the plural so the apostrophe to show possession is placed *after* it.
- The boys' playground was flooded.
- The ladies' cloakroom was closed.
- The waiters' duties were heavy.

Remember to add 'es' to make the plural if the word ends in double 's'.
- The guests complained about the waitresses' poor service.
- The jury listened carefully to the witnesses' detailed testimony.

However, 'for goodness' sake' always omits the extra 's' as it would not be pronounced.

Do *not* use an apostrophe unless the word is showing possession. Do *not* use it because the word ends in 's'.

*Looking at the exceptions*
Some words do not add an 's' to make a plural. In this case the word is treated in the same way as a singular noun. An 's' is added and the apostrophe is placed before it.

Some words whose plurals do not end in 's' are:

| *Singular* | *Plural* |
| --- | --- |
| child | children |
| deer | deer |
| goose | geese |
| louse | lice |
| man | men |
| mouse | mice |
| ox | oxen |
| person | people |
| policeman | policemen |
| sheep | sheep |
| woman | women |

– The children's coats were on the floor.
– The rubber tubes looked like mice's tails.
– The geese's loud cackling was giving her a headache.
– The women's waiting room was closed.
– The policemen's uniforms were badly made.

### Dealing with exceptions

'Its' is a possessive pronoun and never takes an apostrophe.
   It's = it is or it has.
– Its fur was wet (possessive).
– It's (is) very hot today.
– It's (has) been named Bruno.

**Pronouns** are parts of speech which take the place of nouns. Apart from 'mine', the other possessive pronouns are: hers, his, theirs, yours, ours. None of these takes an apostrophe as each already shows possession.
– That book is hers.
– That beautiful house is theirs.
– Ours was the best score.
– Yours has won the race.

## ABBREVIATING WORDS

### Using apostrophes

Apostrophes are also used if words are shortened or combined. The apostrophe replaces the missing letter or letters:

| | |
|---|---|
| cannot | can't |
| could have | could've (not 'of') |
| do not | don't |
| might have | might've |
| shall not | shan't |
| will not | won't |
| would have | would've |
| would not | wouldn't |

## Using the full stop

If a word is abbreviated, a full stop is usually placed at the end to indicate this:

| | |
|---|---|
| adjective | adj. |
| adverb | adv. |
| document | doc. |
| et cetera | etc. |
| including | incl. |
| information | info. |
| language | lang. |
| plural | pl. |
| singular | sing. |

The same thing applies when abbreviating a county:

| | |
|---|---|
| Berkshire | Berks. |
| Buckinghamshire | Bucks. |
| Cambridgeshire | Cambs. |
| Gloucestershire | Glos. |
| Hampshire | Hants. |
| Lancashire | Lancs. |
| Nottinghamshire | Notts. |
| Oxfordshire | Oxon. |

Some titles also require full stops if they are abbreviated. However, in some cases the title should only be abbreviated if it is followed by the person's full name.

Capt. Anthony Wells or Captain Wells
*not*
Capt. Wells

Col. Peter Barrington or Colonel Barrington
*not*
Col. Barrington

Rev. James Bywaters or Reverend Bywaters
*not*
Rev. Bywaters.

Prof. William Reynolds or Professor Reynolds
*not*
Prof. Reynolds

## HANDLING CONTRACTIONS

Words that are abbreviated by using the first and last letters are contractions and do not usually require a full stop at the end:

| Doctor | Dr | |
|---|---|---|
| Miss | Ms | |
| Mister | Mr | |
| Mistress | Mrs | Ms |
| Road | Rd | |
| Saint | St | |
| Street | St | |

## USING ACRONYMS AND OTHER ABBREVIATIONS

**Acronyms** are words formed from the initial letters of other words. These have become so common that it is easy to forget their origin and sometimes they are no longer written in capital letters or with full stops between them:

| AIDS: | Acquired immune deficiency syndrome |
|---|---|
| ANZAC: | Australian and New Zealand Army Corps |
| ASH: | Action on Smoking and Health |
| ERNIE: | Electronic random number indicator equipment (used to select Premium Bonds) |
| GATT: | General Agreement on Tariffs and Trade |
| LAMDA: | London Academy of Music and Dramatic Art |
| LASER: | Light amplification by stimulated emission of radiation |
| NASA: | National Aeronautic and Space Administration |

| | |
|---|---|
| NATO: | North Atlantic Treaty Organisation |
| RADA: | Royal Academy of Dramatic Art |
| RADAR: | Radio detection and ranging |
| RAF: | Royal Air Force |
| SCATS: | Schools', Christian Assembly Teams |
| SCUBA: | Self-contained underwater breathing apparatus |
| SONAR: | Sound navigation and ranging |
| UCCA: | Universities' Central Council on Admissions |
| UNESCO: | United Nations Educational, Scientific and Cultural Organisation |
| VAT: | Value Added Tax |

There are other abbreviations whose initial letters do not form words but the letters themselves are still more familiar than their derivation:

| | |
|---|---|
| AGM: | annual general meeting |
| CPS: | Crown Prosecution Service |
| BBC: | British Broadcasting Corporation |
| GCSE: | General Certificate of Secondary Education |
| POW: | Prisoner of war |
| TUC: | Trades Union Congress |
| TV: | Television |
| MOD: | Ministry of Defence |
| VIP: | Very important person |

## CHECKLIST

- Use apostrophes when a letter is omitted.

- Use apostrophes to show something belongs.

- The apostrophe goes *before* the 's' when the word is singular and *after* the 's' when plural.

- In words that do not end in 's' for the plural, add an 's' and place the apostrophe *before* it.

- 'Its' possessive requires *no apostrophe*.

- Use full stops at the end of abbreviations but not contractions.

- Full stops are no longer necessary in familiar acronyms.

## PRACTISING WHAT YOU'VE LEARNT

Correct the following sentences:

1. The childs ball was thrown into the neighbours garden.

2. The duchess memoirs were published last year.

3. I always buy my paper at the newsagents.

4. Her months annual leave was cancelled.

5. The childrens outing was a great success.

6. James parents were furious.

7. The ladies fashion department was closed.

8. Don't forget your umbrella for goodness sake.

9. We should of won the match.

10. The cat always licks it's fur when it comes in.

11. Her's was the victory.

12. You might of told me you were going to London.

13. The child wouldnt eat her lunch.

14. Dr. Jones went to South St. to visit Rev. Cauldwell at St. Cuthberts Church.

# 8

## Revising the Chapters

This chapter recaps the work that has been covered in the previous seven chapters. The exercise at the end contains a combination of work from all seven chapters.

### IDENTIFYING DIFFERENT SOUNDS

Although there are only 26 letters in the alphabet, there are many more sounds that are formed by the combination of two letters; these are known as diphthongs or digraphs. The vowel is usually pronounced as a short sound when it is between two consonants and long when there is an 'e' at the end of the word.

| Short vowel sounds: | bat | bet | hill | hot | sup |
|---|---|---|---|---|---|
| Long vowel sounds: | hate | cede | bite | hope | tube |

### Producing long 'a' sounds
As well as words which end in 'e', the following combinations of letters are used for long 'a' sounds: ai, ay, ei, ey.

| ai: | hail | grail | tail |
|---|---|---|---|
| ay: | crayon | pay | pray |
| ei: | beige | eight | neighbour |
| ey: | grey | obey | survey |

### Producing the 'e' sounds
The diphthong 'ea' can produce either a short or a long 'e' sound.

| Short 'e': | breath | bread | pleasant | tread |
|---|---|---|---|---|
| Long 'e': | bead | heap | meal | peace |

Other long 'e' sounds are produced by the following combinations: ee, ea, ei, ey, ie.

| ee: | breeze | feel | heel | sleeve |
|---|---|---|---|---|
| ea: | heave | leave | tea | sea |
| ei: | ceiling | deceive | perceive | receive |

| ey: | chimney | donkey | key | monkey |
|-----|---------|--------|-----|--------|
| ie: | brief | field | grieve | siege |

## Producing the 'i' sounds

A short 'i' can be produced by the 'ui' combination:

| biscuit | guilt | guitar |
|---------|-------|--------|

The long 'i' sound can be produced by the following combination of letters: ei, ie, igh.

| ei: | either | height | neither |
|------|--------|--------|---------|
| ie: | lie | pie | tie |
| igh: | fright | right | tight |

## Producing the long 'o' sound

Long 'o' sounds are produced by the following combination of letters: oa, oe, oo, ou, ow, eau.

| oa: | boat | toad | toast |
|------|------|------|-------|
| oe: | doe | foe | woe |
| oo: | brooch | | |
| ou: | boulder | soul | |
| ow: | bow | crow | throw |
| eau: | gateau | | |

## Producing the 'u' sound

A short 'u' can also be produced by ou as in the following:

| double | trouble |
|--------|---------|

## Using the 'y'

A 'y' can be used in the following ways:

- Short 'i' sound: cynic

- Long 'e' sound: happy

- Long 'i' sound: cycle

## Revising other vowel sounds

There are other combinations of letters which produce other vowel sounds:

| 'ar' sound: | bar | car | hard |
|-------------|-----|-----|------|
| 'air' sound: | hair | heir | dare |

| 'ear' sound: | appear | near | beer | career | |
|---|---|---|---|---|---|
| 'er' sound: | teacher | bird | actor | burn | |
| 'oo' sound: | brew | bloom | group | shoe | juice |
| 'oo' sound: | book | wool | | | |
| 'oi' sound: | boil | coil | oil | | |
| 'ou' sound: | about | aloud | allowed | town | |
| 'oy' sound: | alloy | boy | coy | | |
| 'or' sound: | applause | awful | before | boar | bought |
| | call | door | | | |
| 'our' sound: | flour | bough | flower | | |

## Revising the consonant sounds

| ch: | chair | church |
|---|---|---|
| sh: | hush | shake |
| th: | path | these |
| tch: | batch | ditch |

'Ph' is pronounced as an 'f' sound:

photograph          phrase

'Q' is always followed by 'u':

equal          queen          quick

Some consonants are sometimes silent at the beginning of words. These are: g, k, w, p.

gnarled     knew     wreath     pneumonia
psalm

'C' and 'g' can both be pronounced with a hard or a soft sound:

| soft sound: | central | cinema | age | singe |
|---|---|---|---|---|
| hard sound: | cat | care | grate | greed |

## USING CAPITAL LETTERS

Remember to use capital letters for the following:

- after a full stop
- for proper nouns

- for adjectives formed from proper nouns
- for titles of people, plays, books etc.
- for geographical terms.

## REVISING PLURALS

To form a plural, an 's' is usually added to the following types of words:

- Words ending in 'e'

  crone            crones

- Words ending in consonants

  desk             desks

- Words ending in a vowel followed by 'y'

  monkey           monkeys

- The second part of a hyphenated word

  back-bencher     back-benchers.

  'Es' is added to words ending in the following: ss, ch, sh, x, z

  | | | |
  |---|---|---|
  | ss: | ass | asses |
  | ch: | batch | batches |
  | sh: | brush | brushes |
  | x: | box | boxes |
  | z: | waltz | waltzes |

  Some words ending in 'f' change the 'f' to 'v' before adding 'es' for the plural:

  | | | | |
  |---|---|---|---|
  | calf | calves | wolf | wolves |

## CHANGING THE VERB

If other letters have to be added to a verb, the 'y' at the end is sometimes changed into an 'i'.

| worry | worried | | marry | marries |
|-------|---------|---|-------|---------|

It is kept when adding 'ing':

| worry | worrying | | marry | marrying |
|-------|----------|---|-------|----------|

Some verbs change their form for the past tense and the past participle. There is no rule for this so these have to be learnt (refer to Chapter 5).

## ADDING SUFFIXES

Prefixes and suffixes are often added to words to modify their meaning. If adding a suffix to a word ending in 'y', remember that you may have to change the 'y' into an 'i'.

| angry | angrily | | happy | unhappy |
|-------|---------|---|-------|---------|

Don't forget that you usually have to double the consonant at the end of a word before adding a suffix.

| plan | planned | | run | running |
|------|---------|---|-----|---------|

The 'e' at the end of a word usually has to be removed when adding a suffix.

| date | dating | | hope | hoping |
|------|--------|---|------|--------|

## CHECKING THE WORDS

Take care when dealing with homonyms, words that sound the same but are spelt differently. Make sure you are using the correct form of the word. Refer to Chapter 6 to refresh your memory. Don't rely on a spell-check as this will not know which word you require. It will only highlight incorrect spelling.

Learn the list of words near the end of Chapter 6.

## REVISING APOSTROPHES

Apostrophes are used to show that letters have been omitted.

did not            didn't
cannot             can't
would have         would've

They are also used to show possession and an 's' is added.

- The apostrophe goes before the 's' if the word showing possession is singular.
– The boy's book.

- The apostrophe goes after the 's' if the word showing possession is plural.
– The ladies' cloakroom.

Plurals which do not add an 's' are treated the same as singular nouns. An 's' is added and the apostrophe is placed before it.
– The children's coats
– The mice's tails.

Possessive pronouns do not require an apostrophe:

hers     his     its     theirs     yours     ours

Remember that 'its' possessive never has an apostrophe.

## USING ABBREVIATIONS AND CONTRACTIONS

There is a full stop at the end of an abbreviation but not a contraction.

Abbreviation:      information         info.

Contraction:       Doctor              Dr

Many acronyms no longer require a full stop between the letters:

AIDS              LAMDA              NATO

## PRACTISING WHAT YOU'VE REVISED

Correct the following passage:

Sarah dressed carefuly. She knew she looked glamourous. It was a beautifull day when she court the train to london. She opend her handbag although it's clasp was broken. She should of had it mended but she hadnt had time. Inside, she found a leaflet about the schools' exibition. She was dissapointed she would miss it. Their was a seperate sheet containing the childrens' comments. It was quiet humourous because the grammer was so bad and there was alot of mispelling.

The train was beggining to slow down. She hopped Dr. Jones, who was at the top of his proffesion, would see her immediatley she arrived. Taking out her dairy, she checked the time of her apointment which she had enterd as soon as she had recieved the letter.

She new she was early. When she apeared at the door, the secetary asked if she prefered tea or coffee and then left Sarah to read a book of poems which had no ryme or regular rythm. She put it down and stared at the decorative cieling persuing her own thoughts.

# 9

## Exploring the Dictionary

Make time to browse through your dictionary. It can be a fascinating experience and you may be amazed at the variety of information it contains.

### LOOKING AT THE BACKGROUND

Until the fifteenth century all books were hand-written and few people owned one. The Latin Bibles were chained up in the churches and only the priests read from them.

#### Standardising spelling

In 1476 William Caxton introduced the printing press and attempted to standardise the spelling of English. Much of his arbitrary spelling has not survived but it is due to him that the short 'u' sound in some words is now written as an 'o'. Apparently the 'u' on Caxton's primitive printing press was unsatisfactory and he preferred not to use it! The following words probably owe their current spelling to him.

come    done    dove    glove    love    wonder

There were other attempts to standardise and simplify spelling. In the fifteenth century there was an attempt by a monk to make spelling phonetic and in the seventeenth century a bishop attempted a phonetic alphabet. Even in the twentieth century there were unsuccessful attempts to reform spelling. A hilarious paper produced recently suggested our vowel and consonant sounds should be revised to cater for European speakers of English. Among the suggestions were:

- 'c' would be abolished and replaced by 's' or 'k'

- 'ph' would no longer be used instead of 'f'

- the silent 'e' would be dropped

- 'w' should be replaced by 'v'
- 'th' would be replaced by 'z'.

The examples given were unrecognisable as English!

## Compiling a dictionary

Although there was an attempt at compiling rudimentary dictionaries in the Middle Ages, it was not until 1604 that Robert Cawfray produced his *Table Alphabetical* – a rudimentary dictionary intended for 'ladies . . . or any other unskilfull persons'! We do not know how successful this was!

The first dictionaries only contained 'difficult' words, particularly those derived from foreign languages. It was assumed that words in common usage needed no definition. In 1658 Edward Phillips, a nephew of John Milton, produced *New World of English Words*. He described it as 'containing the interpretation of such hard words as are derived from other languages.'

It was in the following century that England followed the pattern set by the Academies of Italy and France and decided to 'purify' the English language. It was felt that, at that time, the language had reached such perfection that it would deteriorate unless it was standardised by a recognised authority. As England had no 'Academy' for this purpose as had Italy and France, the task was given to Dr Samuel Johnson, whose reputation as a man of learning was widely recognised. When he started work, he is said to have found the language 'copious without order and energetick without rules'. He set about changing this!

His dictionary first appeared in 1755 and was the forerunner of those we use today. Unlike some of his contemporaries, Johnson recognised that language was constantly changing. It could not be set in stone and preserved like a museum antiquity. A dictionary has to be frequently updated and, with the advent today of so much new technology, a vast number of words have been added to our vocabulary and have to be included in revised dictionaries. Another name for a dictionary is a lexicon and the compiling of one is called lexicography.

The first edition of the *Oxford English Dictionary* was edited by Sir James Murray between 1884 and 1928. Today this famous dictionary has been computerised.

## Spelling badly is not new!

The introduction of the dictionary did not apparently eradicate bad spelling. In the eighteenth century Susanna Wesley wrote to her son, John, that 'few are taught to *spell* their mother tongue correctly'. She referred scathingly to 'some original letters of lords and ladies . . . where the writing is elegant and the spelling execrable'.

*The Practical Speller* published in 1881 complained that school leavers 'shock society by their bad spelling' and at the end of the century poor spelling apparently caused the majority of failures in a Civil Service examination. Has anything changed at the end of the twentieth century?

## DISCOVERING THE ROOTS OF WORDS

English is a difficult language to learn because so many of its words are derived from other languages. Sometimes words fall into disuse and in this case they are identified in the dictionary by 'arch'. This stands for archaic and means that the word is no longer in use.

The two languages which have contributed most to English are Latin and French.

### Finding Latin contributions

Latin was the language of the mediaeval church and the first 'dictionaries' were attempts by monks in the fifteenth century to produce English equivalent for Latin words. Words that end in 'a' 'i', 'um' and 'us' are often derived from a Latin word. Latin words are still used in the following disciplines today: biology, botany, chemistry, medicine, music, physics.

The following Latin phrases are still in use today:

| | |
|---|---|
| *ad hoc* | – for this purpose |
| *ad infinitum* | – for ever |
| *ad nauseam* | – to an excessive degree |
| *alter ago* | – one's other self |
| *bona fide* | – in good faith |
| *compos mentis* | – sane |
| *curriculum vitae* | – an account of one's career |
| *deus ex machina* | – the unexpected saving of an impossible situation |
| *dramatis personae* | – list of characters in a play |

| | |
|---|---|
| *et alibi* (et al.) | – and elsewhere |
| *et cetera* | – and so on |
| *ex curia* | – not in open court |
| *habeas corpus* | – produce the body (a person must be brought into court) |
| *in absentia* | – while absent |
| *in camera* | – not in open court |
| *infra dig* | – beneath one's dignity |
| *in loco parentis* | – taking the place of a parent |
| *in memoriam* | – in memory |
| *in situ* | – in its original place |
| *magnum opus* | – great work of art |
| *nota bene* | – note well |
| *rigor mortis* | – stiffening of corpse |
| *status quo* | – the same state as at present |
| *terra firma* | – dry land |
| *viva voce* | – oral examination |

## Finding French contributions

After the Norman conquest in 1066 French was introduced into England by the conquerors whose language it was. It became the language of the ruling classes, government and the law. However, the dour Anglo Saxons had no intention of losing their own language and English was still spoken by the natives, but it was inevitable that French words and phrases would creep in and eventually become common usage. A number of words still currently in use are derived from French while some French words and phrases have passed into our language as they are.

*Examples of French words and phrases in common use*

| | |
|---|---|
| *affaire de coeur* | – affair of the heart |
| *agent provacateur* | – someone employed to trap a suspect |
| *aide de camp* | – officer assisting a senior officer |
| *à la carte* | – separate items on a menu |
| *amour propre* | – self-esteem |
| *après-ski* | – done or worn after skiing |
| *au gratin* | – cooked in breadcrumbs and grated cheese |
| *au naturel* | – uncooked |
| *avant-garde* | – new progressive ideas |
| *bête noire* | – a pet aversion |
| *carte blanche* | – full discretionary powers given to a person |

| | |
|---|---|
| *c'est la vie* | – life's like that |
| *chargé d'affaires* | – ambassador's deputy |
| *corps de ballet* | – company of ballet dancers |
| *corps diplomatique* | – diplomatic corps |
| *coup de grace* | – a fatal blow |
| *coup d'état* | – a sudden change in government |
| *cul-de-sac* | – a blind alley |
| *déjà vu* | – a feeling of having experienced something before |
| *en bloc* | – all at the same time |
| *enfant terrible* | – unruly child |
| *en masse* | – all together |
| *en route* | – on the way |
| *en suite* | – forming a single unit |
| *entre nous* | – between us – in private |
| *fait accompli* | – something done that cannot be changed |
| *faute de mieux* | – for lack of something better |
| *faux pas* | – a blunder |
| *femme fatale* | – dangerously attractive woman |
| *hors de combat* | – out of the fight |
| *hors d'oeuvre* | – appetiser before main course |
| *maître d'hotel* | – head waiter |
| *mot juste* | – the right word |
| *noblesse oblige* | – privilege brings responsibility |
| *nom de plume* | – pen name |
| *sang-froid* | – calmness in danger |
| *savoir faire* | – knowing how to behave in any situation |
| *table d'hôte* | – fixed price menu |
| *tête à tête* | – private conversation |
| *objet d'art* | – a work of artistic value |
| *on dit* | – gossip |
| *petit four* | – a small fancy cake |
| *petit mal* | – a mild form of epilepsy |
| *petit point* | – embroidery using small stitches |
| *pot-pourri* | – a mixture |
| *rendezvous* | – a meeting place |
| *tour de force* | – a feat of strength or skill |
| *vis-à-vis* | – face to face |

## Looking at other languages

If you browse through the dictionary you will find many words
which come from all over the world. The British have always been

great travellers and while, on the whole, they do not excel at learning other languages, they have frequently picked up interesting words and phrases which, over the years, have been incorporated into English to make it the rich language it is. Words that are derived from other languages are identified.

At the front of most dictionaries you will find a list of abbreviations that are used in the work. Some of these represent foreign languages. You will be astonished at the variety!

*Abbreviations for foreign languages*

| | | |
|---|---|---|
| Afrik. (Afrikaans) | Arab. (Arabic) | Aram. (Aramaic) |
| Assyr. (Assyrian) | Bret. (Breton) | Burm. (Burmese) |
| Chin. (Chinese) | Dan. (Danish) | F. (French) |
| Flem. (Flemish) | G. (German) | Gael. (Gaelic) |
| Gk. (Greek) | Hung. (Hungarian) | Icel. (Icelandic) |
| It. (Italian) | Jap. (Japanese) | L. (Latin) |
| Pers. (Persian) | Peru. (Peruvian) | Pol. (Polish) |
| Port. (Portuguese) | Skr. (Sanskrit) | Sw. (Swedish) |
| Teut. (Teutonic) | Turk. (Turkish) | |

*Examples of words from other languages*
Here are some words that have originated in other countries:

| | | | | |
|---|---|---|---|---|
| Afrikaans: | apartheid | commando | spoor | trek |
| Arabic: | Algebra | assassin | cipher | cotton |
| | magazine | mattress | tariff | |
| Chinese: | kowtow | silk | tycoon | typhoon |
| Japanese: | geisha | harakiri | judo | karate |
| | kimono | | | |
| Persian: | bazaar | caravan | shawl | taffeta |
| Turkish: | caviar | jackal | kiosk | yoghurt |

## FINDING THE PARTS OF SPEECH

Each word in English is a 'part of speech' and plays a particular part in the sentence. Your dictionary will identify each word for you using the appropriate abbreviation.

*Defining the parts of speech*
To refresh your memory, the parts of speech with their abbreviations are set out below:

- **Noun** (n.): a person, place or thing.

- **Pronoun** (pron.): a word that replaces a noun.

- **Verb** (v.t. and v.i.): an 'action' or 'being' word; v.t. is a transitive verb and takes an object. (It is followed by a noun. 'He wrote a letter': letter=object.) v.i. is an intransitive verb and does not take an object. (It is not followed by a noun. 'She dances beautifully'.) Some verbs can be both transitive and intransitive. Look at the following:
  – (Transitive) She danced the waltz, (waltz = object).
  – (Intransitive) He writes well, (no object).

- **Adjective** (adj.): a word that describes a noun.

- **Adverb** (adv.): a word that qualifies a verb, an adjective or another adverb.

- **Conjunction** (conj.): a word that joins two ideas (clauses) in a sentence.

- **Preposition** (prep.): a word that shows the relationship between one word and another.

## LEARNING PRONUNCIATION

The dictionary will also help you to pronounce words with which you are unfamiliar. Does the stress fall on the first or second syllable? Are there 'silent' letters? Is 'c' pronounced as a 'k'?

### Using 'received pronunciation'

The pronunciation used by most dictionary compilers is known as 'received pronunciation'. It takes no acount of the variations used in different parts of the British Isles or indeed in other parts of the English speaking world although some may refer to American spelling and pronunciation. 'Received pronunciation' is standard English 'without any accent' associated with speakers from the South of England. (Others may, of course, consider this itself is an 'accent'!)

The phonetic pronunciation, where necessary, is shown in brackets:

*Using stress marks*
The symbol ' is used after the stressed vowel:

chron'icle     fo'lder     my'stery     ri'ddle     spo'rran

Short vowel sounds are shown by a little semi-circle above the letter:

băt     bĭtter     bŭtter     chĭn     dŏg     fătten
hŏt     hŏp     lĭt     nŭt

The word 'love' would be shown as (luv).
The same symbol over a 'y' shows that the letter is pronounced as 'ee':

factorў     libertў     happў     prettў

Long vowel sounds have a line over the top:

fāte     hōpe     gō     nōte     nō     nūde
ōde     rāte     rōpe     rōse

A vertical stroke between two letters is sometimes used to identify a syllable (unit of a word).

ine'bri/ate     magne'si/a     medi/ate     nu'cle/us

*Examples of pronunciation*

blun'derbuss     blu'bber     co'ma     fa'ctor
fa'ctual     fa'culty     ha'bit

## CHECKING THE MEANING

On most occasions you will probably use the dictionary either to check the spelling of a word or to find its meaning. The main words will be in alphabetical order in bold type and the definition will follow.

**compel** v.t.          to force
**leather** n.          tanned animal skin

## Adding extra words

Some words have other words and phrases linked to them. In this case the original word is represented by the symbol ~ in bold type and the other words follow – also in bold type. Each has a definition, for instance:

'**wash**' can be followed by other words linked by hyphens:

~-basin ~-bowl ~-house ~-leather

~-pot ~-rag ~-stand ~-tub

~-woman

Expressions using **wash** are also given:

~up won't~ ~ed out ~up

~out

There may also be examples to clarify the meaning. These are usually shown in italics:

– *He was washed overboard.*

– *It was washed up by the sea.*

– *She washed down the tablet with a sip of water.*

## Looking at different meanings

If a word has more than one meaning it will appear more than once in bold type in the margin of the page and the different definitions will be given. Each will usually be a different part of speech.

*Examples*

– anger 1 (n.) extreme displeasure

– anger 2 (v.t.) to make someone angry

– fast 1 (v.i.) to go without food

– fast 2 (n.) the act of going without food

– fast 3 (a.) firmly attached to something

– fast 4 (adv.) quickly

– grate 1 (n.) metal frame holding fuel in a fireplace

– grate 2 (v.t.) to reduce a substance to small pieces by rubbing on a rough surface

– grate 3 (v.i.) to create a harsh sound which has an irritating effect

– land 1 (n.) solid part of earth: a particular country

– land 2 (v.i.) to disembark from a ship or bring a plane down to earth.

## ADDING NEW WORDS

New words are constantly being added to our language. Lewis Carroll is credited with introducing 'portmanteau' words in his children's classic *Alice through the Looking Glass*. 'Portmanteau' words are words that combine two known words:

– chortle: a combination of chuckle and snort.

Today these have become very popular and we have:

| | |
|---|---|
| brunch | – breakfast and lunch |
| medicare | – medical and care |
| motel | – motor and hotel |
| Oxbridge | – Oxford and Cambridge |
| transistor | – transfer and resistor |

### Shortening words
Another modern trend is to shorten words. A syllable is deleted and the 'new' word becomes accepted while its original is often forgotten

| | |
|---|---|
| cello | – violoncello |
| fridge | – refrigerator |
| lunch | – luncheon |
| phone | – telephone |
| taxi | – taxicab |
| wig | – periwig |

## USING THE DICTIONARY

A dictionary, as we have seen, has many uses:

• defines the word

• gives the definition

• indicates the pronunciation

• shows the part of speech.

### Finding other uses
In the front of the book you will find a list of abbreviations used and some notes on how pronunciation is indicated. There will also

be a piece on etymology (the derivation of words) and this will show you how the origins of certain words are identified.

At the back of the dictionary you may also find the following:

- list of the chemical elements

- list of weights and measures

- temperature

- list of world monetary units

- Roman numerals

- countries of the world

- States of the USA

- rulers of England and the UK

- Prime Ministers of Great Britain and the UK

- Presidents of the USA

- books of the Bible

- days of the week and months of the year with their derivations

- signs of the zodiac with an explanation of it

- wedding anniversaries

- terms for some groups of animals and birds

- foreign words and phrases that have passed into our language.

The *Oxford Popular English Dictionary* published in 1998 also contains the following helpful information:

- some points of English usage:
  - pronunciation
  - spellings
  - meanings
  - plurals
  - grammar.

- Punctuation:
  - apostrophe
  - colon

– comma
– dash
– exclamation mark
– full stop
– hyphen
– question mark
– quotation marks
– semicolon.

## Looking at other dictionaries

The *Oxford Dictionary* in its entirety runs to 20 volumes and carries a comprehensive list of words. However, you can also find a number of specialised dictionaries which could be useful if you are studying a particular subject or are interested in language and how it has developed. Below is a list of some of the dictionaries you might find in your local library.

*Dictionary of Jargon*
*Dictionary of Contemporary Slang*
*Rhyming Dictionary*
*Dictionary of New Words*
*Dictionary of Music*
*Dictionary of Chemistry*
*Dictionary of Physics*
*Dictionary of Biology*
*Dictionary of Art and Artists*
*Biographical Dictionary*
*Bible Dictionary*
*Medical Dictionary*
*Dictionary of Abbreviations*
*Dictionary of Foreign Expressions*
*Five Language Technology Dictionary* (English, French, German, Italian, Spanish)

## WIDENING YOUR VOCABULARY

You will increase your vocabulary by reading widely. Make a list of words you don't understand and look them up. Remember to note the context in which they are used or you may become confused. Use them in your own writing or speaking as soon as possible.

## CHECKLIST

- Many English words are derived from a number of different languages.

- Foreign words and phrases are still used.

- A dictionary gives parts of speech, pronunciation, definition and derivation.

## PRACTISING WHAT YOU'VE LEARNT

1. Look up the following words and write down their derivation, part of speech and definition:

   | | | | | |
   |---|---|---|---|---|
   | circus | dunce | entrepreneur | envelope | fossil |
   | nucleus | relaxation | scribble | shock | silicon |

2. What do the following letters stand for?

   n.        adj.        adv.        v.i.        v.t.

# 10

## Discovering the Thesaurus

The word 'thesaurus' comes from a Greek word referring to treasure that is hoarded – an appropriate name for this treasure of a book which will help you to widen your vocabulary and improve your writing by finding **synonyms** to replace well-used words. A synonym is a word which has a similar meaning to another.

### LOOKING AT ROGET AND HIS THESAURUS

Peter Mark Roget produced the first thesaurus. Born in London in 1779, he studied medicine at Edinburgh, went on to become professor of physiology at the Royal Institution and became Secretary of the Royal Society. He was active in founding the University of London and remained on the Senate of the University until his death in 1869.

Early in his career he had compiled a thesaurus for his own use and he completed the first draft in 1806. During the next 40 years he continually added to his list of synonyms. He retired from medical practice in 1840 but it was not until 1849 that he started to concentrate on the work for which he is remembered.

His *Thesaurus of English Words and Phrases* was eventually published by Longmans in 1852. He explained that it was 'classified and arranged so as to facilitate the expression of ideas and assist in literary composition'. Twenty-eight editions were published during his lifetime. The edition of 1879 contains his final work. After his death his son edited the *Thesaurus* and later passed this responsibility on to *his* son. The pattern of the *Thesaurus* is logical and easy to follow. Roget aimed to produce a 'collection of words . . . arranged, not in alphabetical order as they are in a dictionary, but according to the ideas which they express'. He wished 'to find the word or words by which (an) idea may be most fittingly and aptly expressed'.

*Roget's Thesaurus* is still a vital reference book for everyone interested in the English language and, like the dictionary, it is frequently updated. Longman's no longer retain the outright copyright and now other publishers produce their own thesauri.

## USING ROGET'S THESAURUS

*Roget's Thesaurus* is divided into two main parts. The first section of the book is divided into the following classifications:

- abstract relations

- space

- matter

- intellect

- volition

- affection.

The second part is the index which, like a dictionary, is in alphabetical order. You will find all words and phrases followed by numbers which refer to the first section.

### Finding your way around

Your first task will be to look up the word or phrase you wish to replace. Having found it, you will discover a variety of other words below it in italics. Beside each one is a number and the abbreviation which identifies the part of speech. Look up the number of the correct part of speech that you require. When you find it, you will discover the word in bold type. Underneath, also in bold type, is the part of speech. Remember that some words can be used as different parts of speech depending on their context.

Following the abbreviation for the part of speech are a number of synonyms from which you can choose. Cross references to other numbers which are appropriate are also given. The later *Thesauri* may contain over 100,000 words so you have a wide variety from which to choose.

*Example*

'Nice' is a very overworked word. Looking this up in the index will give you a variety of synonyms, all of which are adjectives:

| pleasant | careful | discriminating | accurate |
|----------|---------|----------------|----------|
| clean | beautiful | fastidious | amiable |

Each is followed by a number so that you can find even more related words.

'Beautiful' might be number 841. Turning to this number in the first section of the book, you will find the bold heading is 'beauty' because the noun is usually placed first. Following are a number of synonyms with cross references to other numbers. Below this is the adjective 'beautiful' which you require. Among the synonyms given are:

| lovely | fair | bright | radiant | pretty |
|--------|------|--------|---------|--------|

Here, too, will be cross references to other related words.

Although at first you may find it confusing, persevere and it will soon become easier. You will find you are adding to your vocabulary every time you use the *Thesaurus*.

## CHECKING OTHER THESAURI

Since Longmans no longer have a monopoly on publishing *Roget's Thesaurus*, other publishers have now taken it up and are also publishing their own versions. Sometimes these are combined with a dictionary.

Harper Collins have produced a useful pocket dictionary with 34,000 words and a thesaurus with 75,000 synonyms. It is easy to use as the word in bold type is followed by several synonyms. There may be several uses of the word which are identified.

### Looking at an example
grasp: 1. v. clasp, clutch, grip, bold, seize.
       2. v. understand, comprehend.
       3. n. grip, hold, possession.
       4. n. comprehension, understanding.

### Identifying other pulishers
Oxford University Press and Chambers are two other publishers who produce thesauri but there are others as well. The small pocket editions are useful but are not replacements for *Roget's Thesaurus*.

## WIDENING YOUR VOCABULARY

Browsing through the thesaurus can be an interesting exercise. You can learn many new words in the process. However, the best way to widen your vocabulary is by finding new words to replace ones you have used many times before. Having identified new words, use them.

## CHECKLIST

- A thesaurus helps you to find synonyms for well-used words.

- Some small thesauri are combined with dictionaries.

- Use a thesaurus to widen your vocabulary.

## PRACTISING WHAT YOU'VE LEARNT

1. In the following passage find synonyms for 'nice', without using the same one twice.

   It was a *nice* day so the Browns decided to go for a *nice* picnic. It was *nice* by the sea and they had brought some *nice* food. In the evening they decided to go to a *nice* restaurant and have a *nice* meal. They arrived home late after a *nice* day.

2. Find several synonyms for each of the following words:

   | | | | |
   |---|---|---|---|
   | book (n) | end (v) | freedom (n) | gloomy (adj) |
   | house (n) | laugh (v) | path (n) | play (v) |
   | ship (n) | | | |

# 11

## Enhancing Your Writing

Having sorted out your spelling problems and learned all the uses of the dictionary and thesaurus, you should now be in a position to make your writing more varied and interesting.

### READING WIDELY

The best way of enlarging your vocabulary so that you can improve your writing is to read as much as possible. Try to read a variety of material. By doing so, you will consciously and sub-consciously absorb new words that you can use.

You have to learn words in context. As we have already noticed, many words have several meanings; you have to make sure you are aware of the various ways a word can be used so that you can use it correctly.

#### Keeping up with the news

Try to look at a newspaper every day. You will find the broad-sheets, the larger papers, are likely to provide you with a greater challenge as the vocabulary is more varied than the tabloids, the smaller papers.

| Broadsheets | Tabloids |
|---|---|
| *The Guardian* | *The Daily Mail* |
| *The Independent* | *The Daily Mirror* |
| *The Telegraph* | *News of the World* |
| *Times* | *The Sun* |

Most of the papers produce a Sunday edition; *The Observer* is recognised as the Sunday edition of *The Guardian*.

#### Studying magazines

If you are a magazine addict, try to absorb new words you discover and notice how they are used.

### Enjoying books

Escaping into another world through books is a delightful way of passing the time and it is, of course, mainly from books that you will add to your vocabulary. Vary your reading so that you stretch yourself. Don't always read the same type of book. If you are able to do so, try to have two books available at the same time. One may be for lighter recreational reading, while the other could be a book that needs more concentration.

In both books you will probably find new words. Notice how the writer has used them. Be critical as you read. This does not mean that you are constantly criticising the author. It means that you are looking carefully at how the words and phrases have been used. Has the *mot juste* always been found or do you think a different word would have been more appropriate in the context?

## EXPERIMENTING WITH WORDS

It is essential that you keep a list of each new word you think you might be able to use. It would also be useful to note down the part of speech and give an example of its use. Try to learn two or three new words each day. Write them on cards and put them where you can see them; try to use them as soon as possible. Don't be afraid to try out words you have discovered. If you develop a love of words, your vocabulary will be swiftly enlarged as you become hungry for new additions to it.

### Asking questions

In 1988 *The Oxford University Press* launched *The Oxford Word and Language Service* (OWLS). Its aim was to answer questions about the meaning, origin and use of English words. The service is used by a variety of people, all of whom are fascinated by the English language. OWLS receives hundreds of queries every year and the Oxford Dictionaries team attempts to answer any questions that are thrown at it. So if you have a query about a word to which you cannot find the answer, write to The Oxford University Press at Walton Street, Oxford OX2 6DP.

In 1994 *Questions of English* was published by *The Oxford University Press*. This is a fascinating book which answers questions from lecturers, students, historians, word-game enthusiasts, foreign students, schoolchildren and many others. The questions cover a wide range of topics:

- the origin and meaning of words
- their correct usage
- coined words
- unusual facts about words.

If you are fascinated by the English language, this would be a helpful addition to your library.

## GETTING THE DICTIONARY HABIT

Nothing can replace the use of the dictionary for enlarging your vocabulary. Get into the habit of using it regularly, not only to look up new words but also to discover other meanings of familiar words. Make a note of them for future use and always check the spelling of words that have caused you problems.

### Avoiding Malapropisms

Don't fall into the same trap as Mrs Malaprop, a character in Sheridan's play *The Rivals*. She loved using long words but unfortunately she usually found the wrong one; this resulted in some hilarious expressions. When she objected to one of her nieces' suitors, she told Lydia to 'illiterate' (obliterate) him from her memory. When Lydia starts to object, she exclaims, 'Now don't attempt to extirpate (extricate) yourself from the matter'. Later she explains how she would wish her daughter to be educated:
– She should have a *supercilious* (superficial) knowledge of acounts.
– She should be instructed in *geometry* (geography) so that she might know something about the . . . countries.
– She should be able to *reprehend* (comprehend) the true meaning of what she is saying.
  Words used incorrectly in this way have become known as Malapropisms.

### Avoiding tautologies

A tautology is when the same thing is repeated in different ways.
– The two babies were born simultaneously, at exactly the same time. (Simultaneously means at the same time so you do not need the latter.)
– The prizes were awarded consecutively, one after the other.

(Consecutively means one after the other so the latter phrase is unnecessary.)

## MAKING USE OF THE THESAURUS

The larger your vocabulary, the greater the choice you have when producing your work. Remember that enlarging your vocabulary does not mean that you write more. It means you choose your words more carefully and make sure you are using the correct vocabulary for the piece you are writing.

This is where the thesaurus is invaluable. If you are not happy with your choice of word, you can select the right synonym from a wide range. For those who wish to improve their writing skills, the thesaurus is as important as the dictionary.

### Writing literally

Some pieces of writing are factual and require no 'colour'. They are reports, summaries and straightforward accounts of events. You will need to choose words that convey your message succinctly. Don't pad your work with unnecessary words and expressions. You are writing a literal account with no embroidery.

### Writing figuratively

If you are writing fiction or you wish to evoke the atmosphere of a place or an event, you can use phrases and words to bring your writing to life. We use **figurative** language every day but it is so normal that we are often not aware of it. Any expression that is not *literally* true is figurative. There are a number of figures of speech which produce this language, the most common of which are:

- **Simile**: a comparison using 'like' or 'as'. She looked like a cat who'd swallowed the cream.

- **Metaphor**: an implied comparison. The heat was so intense I was boiling ('boiling' suggests boiling water – obviously not literal).

- **Personification**: giving an inanimate object human characteristics. The wind screamed round the house ('screamed' usually refers to a person; most personification is also metaphorical).

Many metaphorical expressions that are in everyday use become clichés – well-worn phrases. To enhance your writing create your own metaphors and similes.

## CHECKLIST

- Read as widely as possible.
- Note down new words with their meanings.
- Get into the dictionary habit.
- Use the thesaurus to find the right synonym.

# 12

## Looking at American Spelling

American spelling differs from English spelling in a variety of ways. Frequently, nowadays, the American spelling is also given in English dictionaries and in some cases both spellings are now acceptable.

### DOUBLING CONSONANTS – OR NOT

Before a suffix is added, the consonant is often not doubled.

### Dropping the 'l' and the 'p'

Look at the following examples. The 'l' and the 'p' are not doubled as they would be in English spelling.

| English spelling | American spelling |
|---|---|
| annulled | annuled |
| annulling | annuling |
| cancelled | canceled |
| cancelling | canceling |
| handicapped | handicaped |
| handicapping | handicaping |
| kidnapped | kidnaped |
| kidnapper | kidnaper |
| kidnapping | kidnaping |
| panelled | paneled |
| quarrelled | quarreled |
| quarrelling | quarreling |
| signalled | signaled |
| signaller | signaler |
| signalling | signaled |
| travelled | traveled |
| traveller | traveler |
| travelling | traveling |
| worshipped | worshiped |
| worshipper | worshiper |
| worshipping | worshiping |

The following **root word** appears in English dictionaries both with a single 'l' and a double one although the usual English spelling is with a double 'l'. However, when the suffix '-ment' is added, the Americans use a double 'l' while the English use only one.

| Usual English spelling | American spelling |
|---|---|
| install | instal |
| instalment | installment |

In the following words the rule is reversed. The English use a single 'l' while the Americans double it.

| English spelling | American spelling |
|---|---|
| enrol | enroll |
| enthral | enthrall |
| instil | instill |

### Adding an 's'
In some cases an 's' is doubled where the English word would retain the single consonant. In the following cases the American spelling is also accepted in some English dictionaries.

| English spelling | American spelling |
|---|---|
| biased | biassed |
| biasing | biassing |
| focused | focussed |
| focusing | focussing |

### Adding 'ful'
When 'ful' is added to a word that ends in 'll', the double consonant is usually retained in American spelling.

| English spelling | American spelling |
|---|---|
| skilful | skillful |
| fulfil | fullfil |

## IGNORING THE DIPHTHONGS

The ignoring of the 'ae' and 'oe' diphthongs, pioneered by the Americans, is now becoming acceptable in some English words. The 'a' and the 'e' are dropped.

| Original English spelling | American spelling |
| --- | --- |
| anaesthesia | anesthesia |
| anaesthetic | anesthetic |
| archaeology | archeology |
| diarrhoea | diarrhea |
| encyclopaedia | encyclopedia |
| faeces | feces |
| foetus | fetus |
| gynaecology | gynecology |
| manoeuvre | maneuver |
| mediaeval | medieval |
| paediatrician | pediatrician |
| paediatrics | pediatrics |
| palaeography | paleography |
| palaeolithic | paleolithic |

The 'ou' diphthong is not used in the following words. The 'u' is dropped.

| English spelling | American spelling |
| --- | --- |
| mould | mold |
| moult | molt |

## REMOVING THE HYPHEN

When the prefix 'co-' is used, American spelling does not usually include a hyphen even when the root word begins with 'o'.

| English spelling | American spelling |
| --- | --- |
| co-operate | cooperate |
| co-operation | cooperation |
| co-opt | coopt |
| co-ordinate | coordinate |
| co-respondent | corespondent |

## DELETING THE 'U'

In American spelling the 'u' is usually removed if the English word ends in 'our'.

| English spelling | American spelling |
| --- | --- |
| behaviour | behavior |
| candour | candor |

| | |
|---|---|
| clamour | clamor |
| colour | color |
| demeanour | demeanor |
| endeavour | endeavor |
| favourite | favorite |
| flavour | flavor |
| glamour | glamor |
| honour | honor |
| humour | humor |
| labour | labor |
| neighbour | neighbor |
| rancour | rancor |
| rigour | rigor |
| savour | savor |
| succour | succor |
| valour | valor |
| vigour | vigor |

## USING 'ER' INSTEAD OF 'RE'

A number of English words end in 're' but the American spelling usually inverts the two letters.

| English spelling | American spelling |
|---|---|
| calibre | caliber |
| centimetre | centimeter |
| centre | center |
| fibre | fiber |
| goitre | goiter |
| litre | liter |
| lustre | luster |
| manoeuvre | maneuver |
| meagre | meager |
| metre | meter |
| millimetre | millimeter |
| mitre | miter |
| ochre | ocher |
| reconnoitre | reconnoiter |
| sabre | saber |
| sceptre | scepter |
| sombre | somber |

| | |
|---|---|
| spectre | specter |
| theatre | theater |

## USING 'S' INSTEAD OF 'C'

A number of words ending in 'ce' are often spelt 'se' in America.

| *English spelling* | *American spelling* |
|---|---|
| defence | defense |
| offence | offense |
| pretence | pretense |
| vice | vise |

## LOOKING AT OTHER WORDS

There are a number of other words where American spelling differs from English. Look at the following examples.

| *English spelling* | *American spelling* |
|---|---|
| aluminium | aluminum |
| analyse | analyze |
| catalogue | catalog |
| cheque | check |
| curb | kerb |
| dialogue | dialog |
| dived (past tense of dive) | dove |
| got | gotten |
| gauge | gage |
| jewellery | jewelry |
| omelette | omelet |
| paralyse | paralyze |
| to prise open | to prize open |
| privilege | privelege |
| programme | program |
| pyjamas | pajamas |
| speciality | specialty |
| tyre | tire |

### Changing the words

There are also a number of words which are different in America from England. Look at the following examples:

| English word | American word |
|---|---|
| autumn | fall |
| bill | check |
| biscuit | cookie |
| caretaker | janitor |
| crisps | chips |
| cupboard | closet |
| curtains | drapes |
| drawing pin | thumb tack |
| dustbin | garbage can |
| ex-directory | unlisted |
| flat | apartment |
| hair grip | bobby pin |
| holiday | vacation |
| ill | sick |
| lift | elevator |
| lorry | truck |
| nappy | diaper |
| number plate | license plate |
| off-licence | liquor store |
| pavement | sidewalk |
| petrol | gas |
| post | mail |
| pram | baby carriage |
| railway | railroad |
| roundabout | traffic circle |
| shop assistant | sales clerk |
| somewhere | someplace |
| sweets | candy |
| tap | faucet |
| tin | can |
| trousers | pants |
| underground | subway |
| windscreen | windshield |
| zip | zipper |

## CONCLUDING THE CHAPTER

You will see that there are a number of differences. Some are now acceptable for English spelling but if you are unsure about the usage it is safer to use the traditional English spelling. Some American words are also commonly used.

# 13

## Exploring New Words, Jargon and Slang

Language changes all the time and new words and phrases are constantly being added, and words adapted and changed. Yesterday's jargon and slang may well become acceptable and no longer recognised as colloquial.

### COINING NEW WORDS

Words are introduced into the language from many different sources. People and places often give their names to nouns and, with the advent of new technology, many new words have been coined.

### Naming by a person

Many words in the English language are derived from people's names. These are known as **eponyms**. Individuals frequently gave their names to items of clothing with which they were associated. Some food and drink also bears people's names. Other names have also passed into our language.

*Examples*

Bramley: a cooking apple first grown by Matthew Bramley in the mid-nineteenth century.

Benedictine: a liqueur first made by Benedictine monks in the sixteenth century.

Bloomers: the ancestor of women's pants named after American feminist Amelia Jenks Bloomer (1818–1894).

Boycott: to ostracise a person or organisation: Captain Charles Cunningham Boycott was ostracised when he refused to reduce his tenants' rents.

Cardigan: knitted, buttoned jacket named after the seventh Earl of Cardigan, a British Cavalry officer (1797–1868): his men wore the garment in the Crimean War.

Garibaldi: a biscuit with currants named after Italian soldier, Giuseppe Garibaldi (1807–1882).

Leotard: tight, one-piece garment worn by acrobats and dancers: named after the French acrobat, Jules Leotard (1842–1870).

Levis: trademark for a type of jeans named after Levi Strauss, an American immigrant from Bavaria (1830–1902).

Mackintosh: a raincoat named after Scottish chemist, Charles Macintosh (1793–1843) (he did *not* spell his name with a 'k'!).

Pavlova: meringue dessert with cream and fruit named after the Russian ballerina, Anna Pavlova: it was a delicacy created to be served during her ballet tours.

Plimsoll: rubber-soled canvas shoe named after Samuel Plimsoll (1824–98).

Quisling: a traitor who collaborates with the enemy: the Norwegian Vidkum Abraham Quisling (1887–1945) collaborated with the Germans in the Second World War.

Sandwich: two slices of bread separated by a filling: named after the fourth Earl of Sandwich (1718–1792): because he hated to leave the gambling table to eat, his valet brought him beef between two slices of bread.

Saxophone: brass musical instrument named after its Belgian inventor, Adolphe Sax (1814–1894).

Stetson: wide-brimmed felt hat named after the designer, John Batterson Stetson (1830–1906).

Teddy bear: a soft stuffed toy bear named after American President, Theodore (Teddy) Roosevelt (1858–1919): he once saved the life of a bear cub.

Watt: unit of power named after Scottish engineer and inventor, James Watt (1736–1819).

Wellington: waterproof rubber knee boot named after the first Duke of Wellington (1769–1852).

## Naming from a place
Some words take their names from places. This is particularly true of words identifying food and drink. These are called **toponyms** and some examples follow.

*Examples of drink*
Amontillado: a dry sherry originating from the Spanish town of Montilla.

Beaujolais: a red wine produced in the Beaujolais district of France.

Bordeaux: wine from the Bordeaux region of France.

Burgundy: wine produced in the Burgundy region of France.

Champagne: sparkling white wine originally made in the Champagne province of France.

Manhattan: cocktail of whisky, vermouth and bitters originally concocted in Manhattan in the late nineteenth century.

Port: fortified red wine originally produced in the seventeenth century in Oporto in Portugal.

Sherry: fortified Spanish wine originally produced in Jerez in Spain: sherry is a corruption of Jerez.

*Examples of fruit and vegetables*

The following obviously take their names from their place of origin:

| | | | |
|---|---|---|---|
| Brazil nuts | Brussels sprouts | Seville oranges | swede |
| tangerine | | | |

*Examples of cattle*

| | | | |
|---|---|---|---|
| Alderney | Friesian | Guernsey | Hereford |
| Jersey | | | |

*Examples of dogs*

| | | | |
|---|---|---|---|
| Afghan | Alsatian | Labrador | Pekinese |
| Rottweiler | | | |

## ADDING TO THE LANGUAGE

With the advent of new technology there have been many changes during the latter part of the twentieth century. As well as new words, some words have changed their meaning.

### Examples of new words

| | |
|---|---|
| Ageism: n. | discrimination on account of age |
| Aromatherapy: n. | massage using oils |
| Bar code: n. | printed code on shop goods that can be scanned |
| Blitz: n. | devastating attack on something |
| Born-again: adj. | enthusiasm of a new convert – particularly to Christianity |

| | |
|---|---|
| Buyout: n. | a group of managers purchase a company |
| Camcorder: n. | portmanteau word created by the combination of camera and recorder: a portable video: camera combined with a sound recorder |
| Chocoholic: n. | someone who is addicted to chocolate |
| Contraflow: n. | two-way traffic on one carriageway of motorway |
| Credit card: n. | a card which allows customer to spread payments over a period of time |
| Debit card: n. | a card which enables money to be taken automatically from a customer's bank account |
| Designer: adj. | fashionable |
| Desktop publishing: n. | publishing straight from a computer and a laser printer |
| Dinky: n. | an acronym from 'double income, no kids' |
| E-mail: n. | electronic mail sent by computer through a telephone line |
| Ersatz: n. | an artificial substance replacing a natural one |
| Fax: n. v. | printed documents sent via the telephone |
| Flagship: n. | the most important building or item within a group |
| Flak: n. | anti-aircraft fire |
| Green: adj. | used of those who wish to conserve and improve the environment |
| Greenhouse effect: n. | the increase in the earth's temperature |
| Hands-on: adj. | involvement at a personal, practical level |
| Insider trading: n. | illegal buying and selling of shares by those who have inside information |
| Laptop: n. | small personal computer that can be used on the lap |
| Litterbug: n. | someone who is always dropping litter |
| Networking: v. | making business contacts during social engagements |
| New Age: n. | a modern philosophy that suggests the 'old age' has had its day: it combines ideas from various religions |
| Ozone-friendly: adj. | item that does not damage the ozone layer |
| Package-holiday: n. | everything for your holiday is included: travel, hotel, etc. |
| Racism: n. | discrimination on account of race |

| Roadhog: n. | someone who shows no consideration to other road users |
| Sexism: n. | discrimination on account of sex |
| Sound bite: n. | short extract from speech or broadcast |
| State-of-the-art: adj. | up-to-date achievement |
| Tapas: n. | Spanish hors d'oeuvres |
| Toy boy: n. | young male lover of an older woman |
| User-friendly: adj. | easy to understand |
| Workaholic: n. | someone who is addicted to work |

## USING JARGON

The word **jargon** is derived from a Middle English word meaning 'meaningless chatter' or 'babble'. Today the English language would probably be poorer without it as many 'jargon' words and expressions have passed into common usage. The ending of '-ise' on to many words, for example, is obviously here to stay.

marginalise     nationalise     normalise     prioritise     privatise

The Americans have coined a delightful word: quietise – to make quiet.

Jargon expressions pass into the language and often become clichés while we forget their origins. Members of particular groups, professions and organisations have their own jargon but sometimes these are so vivid that they become generally used. Those who play games have their own jargon and so do people who work in the theatre. Members of professions create jargon which is often unintelligible to anyone outside the group.

Many expressions from sport are now in common usage. Look at the following examples.

### Finding sporting images

*From cricket*
– it's not cricket
– knocked for six
– play the game

*From boxing*
– hitting below the belt
– the gloves are off
– saved by the bell

*From football*
– kick into touch
– score an own goal
– move the goalposts.

## Noting jargon words

It is difficult to distinguish between 'new' words and 'jargon' words. Some of the following could have been put in the previous section of 'new' words but the following list may be considered to be more recent words.

| | |
|---|---|
| Down-market: adj. | descriptive of the poor and unsuccessful |
| Headhunter: n. | one who tries to persuade high-flyers to work for his client company |
| In-depth: adj. | detailed |
| Infrastructure: n. | the complete structure of an organisation or institution |
| Input: n. | contribution |
| Feed-back: n. | response to some undertaking or conference |
| Junk food: n. | food with little nutritional value |
| Minder: n. | bodyguard |
| Monetarism: | the philosophy of controlling money in a certain way |
| On going: adj. | continuing |
| Pilot project: n. | the first attempt at a project |
| Political correctness: n. | showing sensitivity to minority groups |
| Pressure group: n. | a group whose aim is to further its particular ideas |
| Quality time: n. | the time devoted by those with careers to their families |
| Real terms (in): n. | the absolute value of something as against the apparent value |
| Recycle: v. | to collect and re-use certain materials |
| Scenario: n. | the conditions in which something can happen |
| Sell-by-date: n. | the date by which a product must be sold |

| | |
|---|---|
| Shelf life: n. | the length of time an article stays on the shop shelf |
| Solvent-abuse: n. | glue sniffing |
| Spin doctor: n. | someone employed (by a politician, for example) to influence public opinion |
| Sub-text: n. | the hidden text that is read between the lines |
| Sweetener: n. | a polite word for a bribe |
| Top up: v. | to supply extra material |
| Tabloid: n. | easy to read small newspaper with many pictures |
| Take on board: v. | to take account of |
| Tactical voting: n. | voting against your own party to prevent another party winning |
| Terminal: adj. | fatal, final |
| Tax haven: n. | a place one can go to avoid paying income tax |
| Up-market: adj. | descriptive of those who are wealthy and successful |
| Zero tolerance: n. | refusing to let anyone get away with anything you consider wrong. |

## EXPLORING SLANG

In one dictionary slang is described as 'colloquial language that rarely lasts long'. It has also been described as very informal language and language that originates from a particular group. Many words become popular for a short period and then disappear without trace; others are local and rarely travel beyond a particular area. However, some words are so evocative that they pass the test of time and sometimes pass into general usage.

There are a number of dictionaries of contemporary slang and, like all dictionaries, these have to be frequently up-dated. Some of them give fascinating insights into the origins of slang terms so if you have some free time you might find a browse through one an enlightening experience.

Following are some examples that are currently used. It is sometimes difficult to distinguish between slang and jargon so some words could probably have fitted into the jargon section of this chapter.

## Examples of slang

| | |
|---|---|
| Ace: adj. | excellent |
| Dozy: adj. | slow witted |
| Auntie: n. | BBC |
| Aussie: n. | an Australian |
| Babe: n. | a sweetheart |
| Bag: n. | an unattractive woman |
| Ballistic: adj. | furious, uncontrolled |
| Bananas: adj. | crazy |
| Banged-up: adj. | imprisoned |
| Baron: n. | a prisoner who exercises power over other inmates |
| Beak: n. | the nose; a person in authority |
| Beatnik: n. | someone following a 'beat' form of dress |
| Beeb: n. | BBC |
| Beef: n./v. | a complaint/to complain |
| Beetle: v. | to hurry |
| Bell: n./v. | a phone call/to telephone |
| Bender: n. | a bout of heavy drinking |
| Biddy: n. | an old woman |
| The Bill: n. | the police |
| Bimbo: n. | an empty-headed woman |
| Bin: v. | to throw away |
| Black Maria: n. | a prison van |
| Blighty: n. | Britain |
| Bloke: n. | a man |
| Blotto: adj. | drunk |
| The blower: n. | the telephone |
| Blown away: v. | killed |
| Blow-out: n. | over-indulgence when eating |
| Cack-handed: adj. | clumsy |
| Chicken: n./adj. | a coward/cowardly |
| Clever-clogs: n. | a know-all |
| Clippie: n. | a bus conductress |
| Cock-up: n. | mistake |
| Dishy: adj. | very attractive |
| Dosh: n. | money |
| Doss: n. | a place to sleep |
| Drop-out: v. | to opt out from normal society |
| n. | someone who opts out |
| Eyeball: v. | to stare |

| | |
|---|---|
| Fab: adj. | wonderful |
| Feisty: adj. | spirited, tough |
| Flash: adj. | ostentatious |
| Flip: v. | to lose control |
| Freebie: n. | a free newspaper or a free item given for promotion purposes |
| Gig: n. | a musical entertainment |
| Glitzy: adj. | glamorous |
| Gob: n. | mouth |
| Gunge: n. | mucky substance |
| Hack: n. | a journalist |
| Hooray Henry: n. | a loud, empty-headed, upper class man |
| Hooter: n. | the nose |
| Hot: adj. | stolen |
| Howler: n. | a bad mistake |
| Iffy: adj. | questionable |
| Keen: adj. | excellent |
| Kip: n. | a short sleep |
| Knees-up: n. | a lively party |
| Kosher: adj. | correct, aceptable |
| Laid back: adj. | very relaxed |
| Leg it: v. | to run away |
| Legless: adj. | drunk |
| Loaded: adj. | very wealthy |
| Lolly: n. | money |
| Loo: n. | the lavatory |
| Loopy: adj. | eccentric |
| Macho: adj. | aggressively masculine |
| Magic: adj. | superlative |
| Mega: adj. | huge, wonderful |
| Monkey suit: n. | a uniform |
| Mug: n. | the face |
| Naff: adj. | shoddy, tasteless |
| Neck: v. | to embrace |
| Oddball: n. | an eccentric person |
| Pad: n. | one's home |
| Parky: adj. | cold |
| Quack: n. | a doctor |
| Recce: n. | a preliminary reconnoitre |
| Rip off: v. | to cheat |
| Sack: n. | a bed |
| Scam: n. | a fraud |

| | |
|---|---|
| Scarper: v. | to run away |
| To shop: v. | to betray someone |
| Shrink: n. | psychiatrist |
| Sleaze: n. | immorality or sordid behaviour |
| Sound: adj. | excellent |
| Spare: adj. | very angry |
| Sprog: n. | a child |
| Spud: n. | a potato |
| Spud-bashing: n. | the peeling of potatoes |
| Stiff: n. | a corpse |
| Swot: n. | a student who works hard |
| Tacky: adj. | shabby |
| Tad: n. adj. adv. | a little, very slightly |
| Tearaway: n. | a reckless young person |
| Tight: adj. | mean with money, miserly |
| Towrag: n. | a person who is regarded with contempt |
| Toff: n. | a socially superior person |
| Togs: n. | clothes |
| Tranny: n. | transistor radio |
| Trick cyclist: n. | psychiatrist |
| Uptight: adj. | tense, stressed |
| Way-out: adj. | extreme, eccentric |
| Wimp: n. | a derogatory term for a timid person |
| Wind-up: n./v. | provocation/to provoke |
| Wrinkly: n. | an old person |
| Zap: v. | to destroy |
| Zilch: n. | nothing |
| Zit: n. | a spot on the skin |

# Suggested Answers

## CHAPTER 1

1. Adding 'ei' or 'ie'
   Believe, brief, ceiling, chief, deceive, eight, freight, grieve, niece, neighbour, priest, protein, receive, rein, seize, sheikh, shield, veil, vein, yield.
2. Correcting the spelling
   a. He opened the biscuit tin but the biscuits were stale.
   b. Neither Jane nor her brother was allowed to go to the match.
   c. She became hysterical when her handbag was stolen.
   d. The doctor was called when the child became ill.
   e. The heir to the throne visited the docks and watched the freight being weighed.
   f. He found the comprehension in his examination paper easy but the translation was more difficult.
   g. The opening of the new station was an impressive occasion.
   h. The group was quiet as the ice slid down the glacier.
   i. There was a spontaneous burst of applause as the winner crossed the finishing line.
   j. The match was abandoned as the pitch was waterlogged.

## CHAPTER 2

Correcting the sentences
1. It was very cold. The crowds were hurrying home.
2. 'How are you?' she asked. 'I haven't seen you for ages.'
3. The roar of the planes grew louder; the boys covered their ears.
4. The English team lost the match.
5. Jobs in the North East are scarce.
6. She only used Persil Automatic in her washing machine.
7. The British Museum was closed for renovation.
8. The group went on a trip on the River Thames.

9. She sent a number of articles to *Woman's Own* but they were returned by the editor, Ms Jenny Ashton.
10. The film *Shakespeare in Love* won seven Oscars.

## CHAPTER 3

1. Plurals

| | | | |
|---|---|---|---|
| alley | alleys | ally | allies |
| baby | babies | chimney | chimneys |
| company | companies | doctor | doctors |
| donkey | donkeys | enemy | enemies |
| enquiry | enquiries | file | files |
| journey | journeys | key | keys |
| lackey | lackeys | niece | nieces |
| nurse | nurses | pencil | pencils |
| pony | ponies | ruby | rubies |
| scene | scenes | sky | skies |
| spray | sprays | storey | storeys |
| story | stories | ticket | tickets |
| tragedy | tragedies | tray | trays |
| trolley | trolleys | victim | victims |
| whale | whales | wheel | wheels |
| whisk | whisks | | |

2. Correcting the sentences
   a. The soldiers were told their courts-martial were to be held the following day.
   b. Comedians often make jokes about their mothers-in-law.
   c. The passers-by ignored the speaker on his soap-box.
   d. All the farmers' wives cut off the mice's tails.
   e. The thieves took the knives from the waiting-rooms.
   f. The leaves turn brown in the autumn and the sheaves of wheat are harvested.
   g. The wolves chased the children who were in fear of their lives.
   h. The sopranos and the contraltos were late for the concert because they couldn't find their librettos.
   i. There were two tornadoes in quick succession.
3. The past tense
   a. She gloried in her misdemeanours.
   b. The examiner remedied the mistake.
   c. The mother worried because her daughter was late home.

  d. The victims of the plague were buried in a mass grave.
  e. Her brother accompanied her to the audition.
  f. They were married last year.

## CHAPTER 4

1. Prefixes

| | |
|---|---|
| ante | before |
| anti | against |
| extra | something outside the 'root' word |
| far | distance of space or time |
| neo | new |

2. Which words need hyphens?
   a. The sub-editor reappeared waving the manuscript which was dotted with semicolons.
   b. When she re-entered, she was accompanied by the vice-chairman.
   c. The vice-admiral criticised the under-secretary for his underhand behaviour.
   d. She could not reach the check-out because of the black-out.
   e. The accident produced a knock-on effect and Jane's car was a write-off.

3. Adding prefixes

| | | | |
|---|---|---|---|
| abridged | unabridged | underact | overact |
| adorned | unadorned | appear | disappear |
| appoint | disappoint | disarm | underarm |
| attached | unattached | broken | unbroken |
| clean | unclean | colon | semicolon |
| conscious | unconscious | create | recreate |
| crowned | uncrowned | final | semifinal |
| hooked | unhooked | laced | unlaced |
| marine | submarine | please | displease |
| title | subtitle | way | subway |

4. Suffixes

| | | | |
|---|---|---|---|
| adorn | adornment | attach | attachment |
| beauty | beautiful | doubt | doubtless (ful) |
| happy | happiness | hate | hateful |
| pain | painful (less) | pity | pitiless (ful) |
| power | powerless (ful) | rest | restful (less) |

## CHAPTER 5

Correct the spellings

She was so *beautiful* that he was *almost* in love with her. He knew she was a *dutiful* daughter but he was *hopeful* that she would *finally* agree to go out with him. He knew she *usually* walked in the park in the morning. When she appeared, he *immediately* went towards her and asked if he could join her. She shook her head *gently* and went on her way. He was *terribly* hurt but realised that she would not *automatically* become his friend. His brain was racing *frantically* as he *planned* his next move and *hoped* she would speak to him.

## CHAPTER 6

Correct the passage

Dick was not *allowed* to go to the *sea*. He wanted to *see* it but he had been *caught* being *rough* with a playmate. He was *bored*. He tried to *write* his *diary* but he was *lonely*. He wanted to *write* a *story* but there was a flash of *lightning* and he had left his *stationery* inside.

The sky was no longer *blue* so he *immediately* ran into the school. He knew the principal would be angry with him. In his class room sat Jacques, the *foreigner*. He was doing some *grammar* exercises but he found *writing sentences* difficult.

*Miserably* Dick sat down. He was not *surprised* that Jacques *misspelled* so many words. He pulled on his *woollen* mitts because his hands were cold.

## CHAPTER 7

Correcting the sentences
1. The child's ball was thrown into the neighbour's (neighbours') garden.
2. The duchess's memoirs were published last year.
3. I always buy my paper at the newsagent's.
4. Her month's annual leave was cancelled.
5. The children's outing was a great success.
6. James' ('s) parents were furious.

7. The ladies' fashion department was closed.
8. Don't forget your umbrella for goodness' sake.
9. We should have ('ve) won the match.
10. The cat always licks its fur when it comes in.
11. Hers was the victory.
12. You might have ('ve) told me you were going to London.
13. The child wouldn't eat her lunch.
14. Dr Jones went to South St to visit Reverend Cauldwell at St Cuthbert's Church.

## CHAPTER 8

Correcting the passage:

Sarah dressed carefully. She knew she looked glamorous. It was a beautiful day when she caught the train to London. She opened her handbag although its clasp was broken. She should've had it mended but she hadn't had time. Inside she found a leaflet about the school's exhibition. She was disappointed she would miss it. There was a separate sheet containing the children's comments. It was quite humorous because the grammar was so bad and there was a lot of misspelling.

The train was beginning to slow down. She hoped Dr Jones, who was at the top of his profession, would see her immediately she arrived. Taking out her diary, she checked the time of her appointment which she had entered as soon as she had received the letter.

She knew she was early. When she appeared at the door, the secretary asked if she preferred tea or coffee and then left Sarah to read a book of poems which had no rhyme or regular rhythm. She put it down and stared at the decorative ceiling pursuing her own thoughts.

## CHAPTER 9

1. Looking up words

circus:        noun, from Latin.
          1. Arena where exhibitions take place.
          2. Travelling show of performing animals, clowns etc.

| | |
|---|---|
| dunce: | noun, from John Duns Scotus whose followers in the fourteenth century were ridiculed as enemies of learning. |
| entrepreneur: | noun, from French. Person in effective control of a business. |
| envelope: | noun, from French. A cover for a letter. |
| fossil: | noun/adjective, from Latin. remains of plant or animal dug up centuries later. |
| nucleus: | noun, from Latin. Central part of something round which others are collected. |
| relaxation: | noun, from Latin. Recreation or cessation from work. |
| scribble: | verb, from Latin. To write hurriedly and carelessly. noun. Careless handwriting. |
| shock: | noun, from French. Sudden physical or mental disturbance. verb. To affect suddenly with a strong emotion. |
| silicon: | noun, from Latin. Non-metallic element. |

2. Abbreviations

n. noun          adj. adjective          adv. adverb
v.i. verb intransitive                v.t. verb transitive

## CHAPTER 10

1. Synonyms

It was a *sunny* day so the Browns decided to go for a *pleasant* picnic. It was *delightful* by the sea and they had brought some *mouth-watering* food. In the evening they decided to go to a *luxurious* restaurant and have a *delicious* meal. They arrived home late after a *lovely* day.

2. Synonyms

| | | | | | |
|---|---|---|---|---|---|
| book: | manual | scroll | tome | tract | volume |
| end: | cease | complete | conclude | finish | terminate |
| freedom: | emancipation | | independence | | liberty |
| gloomy: | depressing shadowy | | dark | dim | overcast |
| house: | abode villa | dwelling cottage | mansion | residence | |

| laugh: | chortle | chuckle | giggle | snigger | |
|--------|---------|---------|--------|---------|--------|
| path:  | avenue  | byway   | road   | route   | street |
| play:  | caper   | gambol  | frolic | revel   | romp   |
| ship:  | boat    | liner   | vessel | yacht   | |

# Glossary

**Abstract noun**. The name of an emotion, state or quality.

**Acronym**. Word formed from the initial letters of other words.

**Adjective**. A word that describes a noun.

**Adverb**. A word that modifies a verb, an adjective or another adverb.

**Cliché**. An overused phrase.

**Compound word**. A word containing more than one syllable.

**Digraph**. Two letters – vowels or consonants – which together produce a single sound.

**Consonants**. All the letters that aren't vowels.

**Diphthong**. Two vowels which together produce a single sound.

**Direct speech**. The actual words spoken by someone.

**Eponyms**. Words derived from someone's name.

**Figurative**. Something that is not literally true.

**Homonyms**. Words that are pronounced the same but spelt differently.

**Homophone**. See homonym.

**Hyphen**. A small dash placed between two words to link them.

**Jargon**. Language used by a particular class or profession.

**Malapropism**. A word that sounds similar but has a different meaning.

**Metaphor**. Implied comparison.

**Noun**. The name of a thing or person.

**Participle**. Part of a verb that can sometimes be used as an adjective but cannot stand alone.

**Past participle**. The part of the verb that can be used with the auxiliary verb 'to have'.

**Personification**. Giving human characteristics to something inanimate.

**Prefix**. Letters placed before the root word to modify its meaning.

**Present participle**. The part of the verb that ends in 'ing'.

**Pronoun**. A word that takes the place of a noun.

**Root word**. The main stem of a word to which can be added other letters.

**Simile**. Comparison using 'like' or 'as'.

**Slang**. Very informal language.

**Spell check**. A program on the computer which highlights incorrect spelling.

**Suffix**. Letters added to the root word to modify its meaning.

**Syllable**. The smallest unit of a word containing at least one vowel.

**Synonym**. A word that is similar in meaning to another word.

**Tautology**. The same thing repeated in different ways.

**Tense**. The verb showing past, present or future.

**Toponyms**. Words derived from a place name.

**Verb**. A 'doing' or 'being' word.

**Vowel**. The vowels are a, e, i, o, u.

# Further Reading

**REFERENCE BOOKS**

*The Wordsworth Book of Spelling Rules*, G. Terry Page (Wordsworth Editions Ltd).

*The Oxford Dictionary for Writers and Editors* (Clarendon Press, Oxford).

*Roget's Thesaurus* (Longman).

*Write Right*, Jan Venolia (David St John).

*Write On!*, Richard Bell and Pauline Bentley (Writers News Ltd).

*Questions of English*, compiled and edited by Jeremy Marshall and Fred McDonald (Oxford University Press).

# Index